OUT OF THE RAT RACE

Out of the Rat Race

A Practical Guide to Taking Control of Your Time and Money So You Can Enjoy Life More

Susan Gregory

Servant Publications
Ann Arbor, Michigan

Vine Books is an imprint of Servant Publications especially
designed to serve evangelical Christians.

Published by Servant Publications
P.O. Box 8617
Ann Arbor, Michigan 48107

Cover design by Multnomah Graphics/Printing

94 95 96 97 98 10 9 8 7 6 5 4 3 2

Printed in the United States of America
ISBN 0-89283-858-2

Library of Congress Cataloging-in-Publication Data

Gregory, Susan, 1950-.
    Out of the rat race : a practical guide to taking control of
your time and money so you can enjoy life more / Susan
Gregory
        p. cm.
    Includes bibliographical references.
    ISBN 0-89283-858-2
    1. Simplicity. 2. Conduct of life. 3. Life style. 4. Quality
of life. I. Title.

Dedication

For Fred—my husband, my partner,
and my traveling companion who lightens my load
and enriches my life journey.

Contents

ACKNOWLEDGMENTS

While I assume full responsibility for any faults within these pages, I am eager to share with many others any commendation this work may justify.

This book would not be if not for the unflagging support of my family, especially Fred, Seth, and Dawit. Thank you for your gift of time and effort so I could devote myself to this project. My faithful and candid friends, especially Dorinda Gier and Mick Fleming, Karmann and Rich Kaplan, Susie Galloway, Karen Griffin, Sharon Persson, Joan Tench and Chris Trautman, lent their experiences, insights, and guidance as found in these pages and in my life.

I send a heartfelt thanks to all who have lent their support for the newsletter: Kitty Lindstrom, Ruth Wolf, Dan O'Neill, and Karen and Jim Gwinn.

For their responsiveness and encouragement, I thank Beth Feia, Ann Spangler, and the staff at Servant Publications. For her sensitivity, alertness, and sharp insights, I thank my editor Liz Heaney (who's not as ruthless as she thinks).

And I especially want to thank my friend and mentor Bob Screen who brought me up through the ranks of writing, who believed in me when I didn't believe in myself, and who freely shared his vast knowledge, principles, and insights about communication and about life.

1

Getting Out of the Rat Race

*The thing about the rat race is that even
if you win, you're still a rat.*

Lily Tomlin

CHANCES ARE YOU WERE BROWSING in a bookstore when the title of this book caught your eye. You read the words *Out of the Rat Race* and your heart leaped. *Oh, wouldn't that be great*, you thought. *I would love to get out of the rat race!*

The rat race! Like most Americans today, you know exactly what it is—not because someone told you about it or because you read a book on it, but because you're living in it. You frequently find yourself feeling exhausted, overwhelmed and out of control. Your goal is simply to survive another day!

Millions of mothers, fathers, wives, husbands, singles, retirees, professionals, laborers and even children are deeply entrenched in a daily rat race. And they'd desperately like to get out.

THE WAY OUT

I spent many years bumbling through life trying to survive the rat race. But finally, I couldn't take it anymore. My turning point came on a December morning in 1990. As often happened, I awoke from a full night's sleep still feeling exhausted. The day ahead was filled with demands for my time, energy and emotions. As a wife, mother, daughter, sister, friend, employer, consultant, and volunteer, I had a full plate. On this particular morning, the mere thought of all my responsibilities felt like a five hundred-pound weight dropped squarely on my shoulders.

The rest of the family stayed nestled in their beds while I stumbled down the stairs to make some coffee and scan the headlines of the morning newspaper. I quickly flipped the pages as I waited for the coffee to brew. About halfway through, my eyes were drawn to a headline on the front page of the Living Section: "Less Is More: Seminar Group Preaches Gospel of Frugal Living." Experience already had taught me some of the benefits of living on less. I knew simple living was less complicated and less stressful than my current lifestyle—it sounded exactly like what I needed. So I read on.

The article highlighted the lives of four professional couples or individuals from various backgrounds and diverse ages. Each had spent many years living high on the hog while they earned lots of money—and yet, like most credit-happy Americans, they spent even more than they made. Even with all the things they accumulated, their lives were anxiety-ridden and meaningless. Exhausted and unhappy, they searched desperately for relief... and at last each of them found what they were looking for at a seminar on frugal, debt-free living and achieving financial independence. Subsequently each person had adopted a new way of life. They were spending less, paying off debt and making plans to retire early and do some travel, do volunteer work full-time, or fulfill some other lifetime dream.

As I read the article, I felt my heart swelling with hope. *I need this kind of change in my life*, I thought. The article ended with an address where readers could mail orders for a cassette tape series on frugal living.[1]

Immediately I sat down at my desk, wrote out a check for

the specified amount and scribbled: "I'm exhausted and I need help now! Please send the tapes as soon as possible. Signed, Desperately Seeking Susan." I put the note and my check in an envelope, addressed and stamped it, and took it to my mailbox. Already I felt a little relief. I then proceeded with my busy, demanding day.

Whoever read my request must have understood my plight because two days later the UPS truck pulled up and the delivery man left the tapes on my porch. After we had listened to all the tapes, my husband and I agreed we needed to make changes in the way we handled our finances. We looked at our spending habits and our priorities and tried to bring the two into better harmony. We decided to make most buying decisions on the basis of need rather than want. We also reviewed the purchases we had made over the last several months to see if they had been "worth it."

> *"My life was like a CRAZY QUILT, a pattern I hated. Hundreds of scattered, unrelated, stimulating fragments, each going off in its own direction, creating a lot of frantic energy. There was no overall structure to hold the pieces together. The Crazy Quilt was a perfect metaphor for my life."* [2]
>
> **Sue Bender**

The first area we tackled was clothes. Both of us like and enjoy nice clothes; we like to dress professionally and in fashion. We teach our children to dress nicely. But when we looked at our spending history, we realized we were spending thousands of dollars on clothes every year! Did we really need more clothes? No. Both of us had plenty of nice clothes in good condition. So we made a pact: We will purchase no clothes for one year.

We kept our commitment and spent no money on clothes

for the next twelve months—except for purchasing underwear (wearing holey undergarments was beyond the call of duty!). The money we saved was redirected to paying off debts, adding to our savings or spending on income-producing investments.

These changes marked the first steps for our family's journey out of the rat race.

LEARNING TO LIVE INTENTIONALLY

While this change made a significant difference in our attitudes about money, we knew that stepping out of the rat race meant more than responsibly managing our financial resources. We started looking at our activities, our busyness, our goals in life and our priorities. We examined the underlying reasons and attitudes which directed our actions. We started being more thoughtful, deliberate and intentional about what we did.

Before long, our once stress-filled lives began to slow down. We learned more about who we were as individuals and as a family. We investigated our personal hopes and the desires of our hearts. We allowed ourselves to dream about the future and plan for a more meaningful, fulfilling life.

After finishing a room in our basement, I closed my downtown office and moved my consulting business—along with desks, chairs, file cabinets, book shelves, computer, fax machine and modem—to my home. Since I no longer carried the overhead costs of office space, employees and other related business expenses, I was able to reduce my client load by half. I bought a cellular telephone so my clients could reach me when I was between appointments, and I took up the duties of bookkeeping, filing, coordinating and other tasks normally completed by my assistant.

Meanwhile, our entire family cut back on living expenses.

We stopped going out to dinner and started making creative meals at home. We replaced recreational shopping with working on art projects, visiting friends or spending time as a family. I didn't need as many business clothes, so our wardrobe budget continued to shrink.

As we underwent this change, naturally our friends noticed the difference. We started talking about our new direction and how much better we felt. Soon, a few of our friends started looking at their lives and began changing some of their spending and consuming habits, too. When we got together, our conversations frequently turned to ways we could order our lives for more enjoyment and less stress.

> *"Bill and I are trying to cut back. We just don't have enough money."* —working mother whose annual salary is $85,000+

About a year later, a friend said, "Susan, you're a writer. Why don't you put together a newsletter about all these ideas? There are so many people who feel overwhelmed with life and who also want out of the rat race, but they don't know where to begin."

I tossed around the idea of publishing a newsletter for several months, then finally developed a prototype for a simple, eight-page monthly newsletter called *Out of the Rat Race*. I printed one hundred copies at my neighborhood copy center and sent them to friends and business associates. To my delight and surprise, more than 50 percent of the people who received my initial mailing subscribed! I was on my way!

People started talking about *Out of the Rat Race*. Television, radio, magazine and newspaper reporters began calling and running stories about the newsletters and how people could redirect their lives. Groups asked me to speak and present workshops. More and more men and women wanted to escape the grind and looked to my simple, eight-page monthly newsletter as their personal support group to help them make their way out of the rat race and on to more fulfilled, enriched lives.

WHERE ARE WE GOING?

Getting out of the rat race does not require a diet of granola and tofu, a wardrobe planned around Birkenstock sandals and heavy woolen socks or selling all your worldly possessions and moving to a little farm in the country. It doesn't mean quitting your job or turning the clock back to the "good old days."

For those of you who want to make the journey, escaping the rat race calls you to learn about yourself; to unveil the very unique and intentionally created being called YOU and to discover your special gifts, talents and life purpose. Turning away from the rat race means ordering your life in such a way that you invest your best time, energy, and resources in those values that are most important to you. It means you must discover who you are and what you want. Soon

> "Never before have I been so tired. I'm so exhausted that I have to take sleeping pills just to get to sleep."
>
> —working mother of a toddler

you will uncover beautiful treasures such as confidence, inner peace, personal achievement and a very special-yet-quiet joy.

The following chapters will serve as your trail guide and take you through ten steps that will help you leave the rat race.

Safe travel out of the rat race requires preparation, for this is a long hike, a path we may have to travel for several years or even decades. We may want to learn a new skill or change our career path. We may have large debts to erase or personal challenges to overcome. Or our family circumstances may require us to take a slower pace.

Thankfully, there is no one behind us barking orders or forcing us to do anything we don't want to do. Our journey is all ours. We choose our own pace and make our own decisions about the paths we want to follow. The path I chose may be different from the one that's right for you. If we stumble along the way or move back into the rat race, we can always start again.

For now, as you begin your escape, let me pass on to you a travel blessing for a safe and heartfelt journey:

May you be encouraged as you begin your journey toward a simple, sincere, and serene life. May you fend off promptly every thought of anxiety, discouragement, and worry while cultivating cheerfulness, charity, and the habit of inner silence. And may you accept the gifts of strength, wisdom, and joy which are available to you in abundance from your Creator.

Happy trails to you from your traveling companion,

Susan

2

The Unveiling

Until we recognize that life is not just something to be enjoyed but rather a task that each of us is assigned, we'll never find meaning in our lives and we'll never be truly happy.[1]

Victor Frankl

CLASS DIDN'T START FOR THIRTY MORE MINUTES. Our nine-year-old adopted son from Ethiopia, Dawit, had plenty of time to walk the eight blocks between our home and his school. He gathered his books and packed them snugly into his slightly-worn book bag. Then he looked up to me with a modest degree of urgency, "Oh Momma, I'm supposed to bring a sample of music I like to listen to and share it with my music class. Can you help me?"

"Sure," I said. I opened the cupboard where we store our tapes and CDs and started flipping through our collection of contemporary, jazz, classical, and light music, most of which was unfamiliar to Dawit since he had come from Ethiopia only eighteen months before.

"This would be good," I said. "It's Ladysmith Black Mombaza." I pulled out the CD of the African group which had gained worldwide notoriety after playing with Paul Simon on his best-selling *Graceland* album. Dawit liked the African style of music and the Zulu lyrics. "This would be great. They're good musicians and you could share with the kids in your class about the different music of the African people."

Dawit didn't respond. As I read through the list of song titles, I glanced over at my son. I was puzzled to see tears falling down his brown cheeks. "Dawit, what's wrong?"

"Oh Momma, I don't want to take African music. The kids at school laugh at me because I'm from Africa."

As I witnessed my son's pain, I felt as if someone was piercing my own heart. This wasn't the first time our family had to deal with racial issues—two of our four children are of color. But, still, it hurts every time.

I wrapped my arms around Dawit and wiped away his tears. I collected my thoughts, then said, "Honey, you don't have to take African music. We have lots of other music you like. Let's look for something else." I started leafing through our other CDs, then gently went on, "But you know, I think we need to talk about the kids laughing at you and how you feel about that."

Dawit remained quiet.

"Dawit, do you think God made a mistake when he made you black?" Dawit's deep trust in God helped him bear the loss of his family when they all died of disease, leaving him alone and homeless for more than a year until the director of an orphanage found him just before his sixth birthday. "No," he replied. "I don't think he made a mistake."

"Do you think he made a mistake when he made me white?"
"No."

"Do you think God made white people better than black people? Or black people better than white people?"
"No."

"Do you think he always knows exactly what he's doing when he creates people?"
"Yes."

"Does God ever make mistakes?"
"No."

"Well then it seems to me those kids who are laughing at you are the ones making the mistake. They're wrong if they think people from Africa should be laughed at. I can understand how sad you feel, but let's make sure we keep thinking about how special God made you and how special he made me and about how special he made every living thing."

I could see Dawit cheering up as he drew comfort from the truth of God's love for him.

"Honey, the people in Africa are different from people here in America. Just like Americans are different from Europeans. Different is okay. In fact, different is good. God doesn't want us all to look the same. That would be boring and God is more creative than that! Do you understand what I'm saying?"

"Yes, Momma. I know God made everyone good even though we don't look the same or talk the same."

"That's right," I agreed. "And we need to help the children who think it's OK to laugh at other people to understand that differences are good—that everyone is different in some ways. We need to help them understand that God wants us all to be different because he has a special purpose for each one of us. And he wants us to accept everyone as special creations of his—not better or worse or mistakes."

Dawit decided to take the *Graceland* album and play a song with Ladysmith Black Mombaza and Paul Simon singing the lyrics together. As he packed the CD into his backpack, Dawit said, "You know, that's the way we should try to be. Different people singing together. Right, Momma?"

Out of the mouths of babes. This time the tears were coming from my eyes.

EACH LIFE IS UNIQUELY AND INTENTIONALLY CREATED BY GOD

That September morning is still vivid in my memory. As he had done many times before, Dawit blessed me with his sensible and guileless wisdom and he confirmed for me once again how important it is that we see all people as God's unique creations. This perspective contains three foundational truths.

The first truth forms the foundation for all others: *God is for real*. Studies show that nine out of ten Americans believe in God. In fact, current trends indicate that Americans are placing an increased emphasis on spiritual values and are turning to churches and synagogues for teaching.

The famed Swiss psychoanalyst Carl Jung is considered to be one of the most astute thinkers and greatest scientists of our time. By comparing his early writings about God with those from his later years, one can see a change in Jung's understanding of God as he journeyed through life.

When Jung was well along in years, an interviewer asked, "Dr. Jung, a lot of your writing has a religious flavor. Do you believe in God?"

Jung responded by saying, "Believe in God? Well, we use the word 'believe' when we think that something is true but we don't yet have a substantial body of evidence to support it. No, I don't believe in God. I know there's a God."[2]

I, too, know there is a God. He is the Creator of the heavens, of the earth and of every living thing.

The second truth is that God *intentionally* created each and every one of us. That means he had an end in mind when he decided to form you, me, your neighbor, your children, your spouse. The psalmist wrote, "Your hands made me and formed me" (Psalm 119:73). Think about potters or sculptors and how personal and caring is the act of making something with one's hands. The writer depicts God as our sculptor. "For you created my inmost being; you knit me together in my mother's womb. I praise you because I am fearfully and wonderfully made" (Psalm 139:14).

The same God who created the planets, the Grand Canyon, and lions and tigers and bears (oh, my), created you and me. That's awesome! Of course, some of us believe he also created world wonders other than the seven recognized the world over—such as burnt creme, Jamocha Almond Fudge ice cream, and major-league baseball (notice I used the word "believe"; I'm still working on the substantial evidence).

The third truth is that *God doesn't make mistakes.* It doesn't take a rocket scientist to see that we are all unique, different, varied. Picture in your mind some of the people you know. As you canvass their faces, immediately you see each one is unique. God creates humankind in a kaleidoscope of colors. We're adorned by multicolored locks, with eyes in varying shades of brilliance. We're tall. We're short. We're lanky. We're round. We're boisterous. We're serious.

> God intentionally created each and every one of us. That means he had an end in mind when he decided to form you, me, your neighbor, your children, your spouse.

I have to admit, I would have loved it if God had given me legs like Tina Turner. And I'm now realizing he doesn't intend for me to age like Jane Fonda, Raquel Welch, or Sophia Loren (how in the world can those women look the way they do and still be blowing out more than fifty candles on their birthday cakes?).

In God's perfect wisdom, he has a reason for each of us. As the French would say, a *raison d'être*, a reason for being. He makes each of us unique. We are designed to achieve an objective, and God gives us everything we need to accomplish that purpose and bring meaning, satisfaction and fulfillment to our lives.

Our individuality and uniqueness is enough reason for not expecting one another to be the same, want the same things, or act the same ways. What is right for me may not be right for you. Because each of us is designed differently, a blanket statement such as "women shouldn't work outside the home" is fraught with error. Our uniqueness accounts for both our strengths and weaknesses and explains why we need one another. Because each of us are distinctive people, we shouldn't try to make others like ourselves or try to be like everyone else.

THEN WHY DO WE STILL TRY TO KEEP UP WITH THE JONESES?

The very Creator of the universe forms us for a purpose and somehow we don't take the opportunity to follow his lead. We don't use his blueprint for our lives so we can become the very best we can be. Instead, we try to fit a mold created by our American or Western society. Why?

Many of us have tried to obtain the American Dream (a.k.a.

Average Daily Television Viewing
(per household)

AVERAGE HOURS	
YEAR	PER DAY
1960	5:06
1965	5:29
1970	5:56
1975	6:07
1980	6:36
1985	7:07
1990	6:55
1992	7:04

Source: Nielsen Television Research [3]

life-better-than-our-parents). When we were growing up, the American Dream meant a husband, a wife, 2.2 children, a dog, and a house in the suburbs with a station wagon in the garage.

But over the last twenty or so years, that model has been updated. Now it includes another car in the garage (which means you need a bigger house with a bigger garage). It means electronic devices in every room, including big screen TVs for the family room, little TVs for the kitchen and the workout room, and yet another TV in the master bedroom (all of these sets are hooked up to VCRs just in case we can't find anything interesting to watch on one of the thirty-five cable stations offered in our area).

The updated American Dream also means telephone answering machines, at least one personal computer loaded with a variety of sophisticated (and sometimes gruesome) games, and Nintendo games in every room where children prowl.

Since we still haven't figured out how to grow money on trees, we strive to earn more dollars in order to secure the illusive American Dream. We need another income for an even bigger house with walk-in closets off our master bedroom to store all the clothes we need to dress for success.

The house, packed full of expensive furnishings, is empty for fifty or sixty hours each week, leaving it a prime target for break-ins (by people who chose another way to secure the American Dream until money starts growing on trees). So we need a motion-sensitive alarm system that sounds as soon as someone stirs in the house without first punching in the right access code.

Where has all this gotten us? Smack dab in the middle of the rat race. Sadly, most of us got there without even knowing we were headed in that direction!

We started climbing the mountain of success to reach the new and improved American Dream and ended up falling in the depths of hustle and bustle, broken relationships, excessive stress and despair. Our egos got tied to the organizational chart of our employers. Our self-worth was defined by the clothes we wore and the car we drove. The quality of our lives was measured by the things we owned.

We became card-carrying members of the rat race.

Many have lost sight of what they really want. They have lost sight of what brings them true happiness. The dreams and passions have faded. And they don't slow down or look back long enough to discover what their real purpose in life is all about.

ACCOMPLISHED... YET CRUMBLING

When I first met Megan she was a picture of success. She scampered up her career ladder and was a recognized leader in her field of work as well as in her community. A mutual friend arranged our meeting. "Professionally, Megan is a very accomplished woman," he told me. "But she's crumbling inside and she doesn't seem to have anyone to talk to. I've convinced her that you can be trusted. Can you meet with her?"

Megan walked into the restaurant where we arranged to meet. I recognized her from my friend's description. Megan was dressed in a tailored, expensive suit which was accessorized just right. Her make-up and hair were perfect and she walked with poise and confidence.

Megan told me her story. After graduating from college in 1972 and starting her career in advertising, Megan married and started a family. She took several weeks off when her baby son arrived but then found suitable daycare.

Megan's husband assumed primary responsibility for their home and son which freed her to devote more time to work. She quickly advanced in her company, and by 1985, Megan and her husband agreed it was time for her to start her own business. She landed several impressive accounts. Soon Megan was invited to sit on several civic boards and started advising many of the community's key business and government leaders.

Still, Megan didn't feel fulfilled. She wanted more of something... but what?

Megan was looking for purpose in all the wrong places. Her story is common today. Like Megan, many of us get caught doing a lot of things right... but still we feel unfulfilled because we're not doing the right things.

When I asked about her marriage and family life, a veil of sadness fell over Megan's face. She began explaining her frustration and resentment about her husband and her son. "I feel as if I'm in a different world than they are," she explained. "I make a lot more money than my husband. I realize he stepped back so I could move ahead. But we just don't relate any more. We're so different. I don't feel like I can take him or my son around the people I associate with in my work. My husband and son just don't have the same interests as my friends."

> "Here [in the forest] every bird and fish knew its course. Every tree had its own place on earth. Only man had lost his way."[4]
>
> **Margaret Craven**

Megan was more attracted to her business associates than she was to her family. Yet she was about to pour her heart out to a stranger because she felt she had no one she could talk to. She couldn't take off her masks and reveal her *real* self to anyone.

Megan admitted feeling confused, overwhelmed and angry about her life. She inventoried her stockpile of achievements, including a doctorate degree, ownership of a successful company, the admiration of peers, a six-figure income, an active social life and a suburban house full of lovely furniture and expensive art. "But if I'm so successful," she said, somewhat perplexed, "why do I feel like I have to do more and more and more to be truly satisfied?"

A lot of people are asking the same questions Megan asked me. A nationwide survey in 1993 revealed that American men and women are ready to trade money for time and prestige for fulfillment. Some are throwing in the towel and moving to the country. Others are foregoing raises and promotions in exchange for more vacation time. Many want out—they just don't know how to get there.

My time with Megan was drawing to a close, but I wanted to give her some things to think about. I decided to ask the sixty-four thousand dollar question: "Megan, have you thought about your life purpose? In other words, why are you doing all that you do? What do you think about your reason for being?"

I could tell by her expression that my query aroused her curiosity. "Well, to be happy, I guess," she said, obviously not satisfied with her response. "I don't know that I've ever thought about my purpose in life."

DISCOVERING OUR LIFE PURPOSE

When was the last time you thought about your purpose in life? For most of us, it is a question we rarely confront—yet failing to identify it causes us great anxiety.

I remember conducting an all-day workshop for men and women who wanted out of the rat race. An elderly woman named Fran was attending. When we reached the subject of life purpose, I asked if there were members in the audience who thought they knew their purpose for living. As I had expected, the room fell silent. When the silence got a little uncomfortable, a few tried to answer. "My purpose is to be a good husband and father," said a young man. A woman of forty or so said, "I have several purposes, like being a good mother, a good wife, a good worker, a good citizen." Then Fran, who appeared to be around seventy years old, raised her hand. In her soft, slightly quivering voice, she said, "I don't have a purpose in life anymore. My children are all grown. I never worked outside our home and my husband died five years ago. I've outlived my purpose for being here."

All eyes turned to me asking, "How can you answer that?" Actually, I couldn't have planned a better set-up.

I thanked the two others for offering their answers, but then explained why their responses were examples of goals or activities and not really of purpose. Many of us confuse our life purpose with our goals or activities. So when we achieve our goals—or worse yet, if we fail at them—we feel as if the bottom has dropped out of our lives.

I once read an article about the tremendous sense of loss and emptiness United States presidents feel after they leave office. Many said they felt as if there were nothing left for them to

> "We all live with the objective of being happy; our lives are all different and yet the same."[5]
>
> **Anne Frank**

do in life. They had reached their highest goal and now felt life had little meaning.

Our life purpose is something we will never outgrow because it will never be achieved in this lifetime. It isn't as specific as "be a good parent" or "become president of the United States" or even "build a better mouse trap." Our purpose is not something we invent, it's something we discover. Our purpose comes from who we are. And that is the good news I was able to give Fran.

A VOICE IN THE WILDERNESS

Victor Frankl, born in Vienna in 1905, is a world-famous psychiatrist. As a Jew he was imprisoned for several years during World War II in the Nazi death camps at Auschwitz and Dachau where his mother, father, wife, and all but one of his siblings were incinerated in the ovens. Frankl endured inhumane treatment month after month, but survived.

Years after his release from the camps he joined the staff at the University of Vienna and there wrote about his own search for a meaningful life amid the horrors of the death camps. His research and work concerning life's meaning evolved into his theory known as *logotheraphy*. Frankl maintains that essential to our humanity is our awareness, conscious or unconscious, of God within us and that our most fundamental motive is to find meaning in life.

Frankl writes, "Until we recognize that life is not just something to be enjoyed but rather a task that each of us is assigned, we'll never find meaning in our lives and we'll never be truly happy."[6]

While NASA's astronauts journey into outer space, some of us are on a journey of our own—a journey in what I call inner space. This is discovering our very deepest thoughts and feelings. It is where our soul presides. It is where the God who is in us lives.

One of the most effective ways of traveling in inner space is through writing and journaling. That's why I encourage you to write your thoughts down as you make your journey out of the rat race.

Find a quiet time in a relaxing environment. Seat yourself in a comfortable chair, lean against a tree as you sit on soft grass, or perch yourself on the banks of a lake or the sea. Begin writing your thoughts. Write to God. Write to yourself. Pour out your heart upon the pages. Dream. Explore. Venture out. Then come around by asking yourself how to respond to all you have written. What will you do? How will you act? This is your time to learn, to grow and to settle on what you believe to be true.

Frankl also taught that when we understand the "why" of our existence we will have much less trouble with the "how" of our lives.

Frankl's theory has yet to be embraced by all of those in the psychiatric profession, but his belief seems to be bearing out. Many experts believe the most significant trend of the '90s is a widespread search for meaning.[7]

PACK YOUR BAGS

Discovering our purpose requires us first to examine ourselves. Who are we? What are our gifts? By what principles do we live? What passions are in our hearts? For what or for whom are we responsible? As Frankl pointed out, discovering our purpose, learning *why* we exist, helps us determine *how* to exist.

As you begin to remove the shrouds you've donned over the years and start seeing yourself in your natural state, you will be taking your first steps in your personal journey. You will begin your treasure hunt in the land of rich and wonderful discovery as you begin to look into your own heart and soul.

Before you start, there are a few things you need to gather for your backpack:

1. *Three-Ring Notebook (Your Personal Travel Log).* I suggest one with 1 1/2" rings that holds 8 1/2" x 11" notebook paper. You may want to choose one in a color that reflects something of your personality, or you may choose the kind with the clear acetate pocket on the cover allowing you to slip in photographs, drawings, poems, or other pieces that have special meaning to you.

2. *Five Tab Dividers.* You will divide your Personal Travel Log into five sections. As you work through this book, you'll answer questions, gather data, and begin discovering valu-

able information about a very special and unique person—YOU! You will continue to use your Travel Log long after you have completed this book. You are developing what may become the most useful guide you will ever create.

Label each of the five sections using these words in this order:

Who I Am
What I Want
How I Want to Live
Facts of Life
Onward and Godward

3. *Paper.* As you make your way out of the rat race, you'll gather valuable information about you and your life. You'll uncover your hopes and dreams for your future. You'll write about what you want to achieve in your lifetime. You'll examine your beliefs and life principles. You'll also investigate your finances and develop a spending plan that's right for you. You'll design a blueprint for your life.

The easiest and most efficient way to keep your information in order is to capture all your thoughts and data on 8 1/2" x 11" paper. I keep at least fifty blank sheets of college-ruled notebook paper in my notebook so it is always available. I also keep a few reams of notebook paper on hand in my office and home. When I need a copy of something to add to my notebook, I duplicate it on 8 1/2" x 11" paper (no matter what its original size might be). And if for some reason I need to file a scrap of paper that is small, I merely tape or glue stick it onto another sheet of 8 1/2" x 11" paper.

Note: *I learned about collecting information from professional researchers who gather mass quantities of data from various sources. It's by far the best, most efficient system I've ever come across—and it's easy!*

4. *Pencils.* I like to use mechanical pencils because they never need sharpening and they feel better in my hand than the wood #2s. Gather or purchase pencils that you like to use and keep them with your notebook. I also like to use colored pencils to underline important facts or truths I discover along the way. Sometimes, I'll add sketches or include little shapes and drawings when I'm journaling or planning.

You now have everything you need to get started. You'll also gather other articles for your pack as you continue your journey.

If you are especially eager to begin your trek and you don't have a notebook or dividers, just start writing your log on 8 1/2" x 11" paper that can be added to your notebook later.

YOUR TURN

Reserve some quiet time to relax and remember. If you're able, go away for a weekend to a serene place where you will feel safe and refreshed. Or take a few hours and visit a park, a gallery, or any special place where you're able to become quiet to allow your heart and soul some breathing room. If you're able to do that at home—perhaps in the early morning or during a mid-day break—then that will work as well.

Use your notebook to record the imprints on your heart. Write as much as you like. The important thing is fleshing out what is significant to you.

You'll reflect on your earlier years and start to see patterns of activities to which you're attracted. Stay positive, recall those situations, achievements and circumstances that have shaped you. Your experiences won't be earth-shaking, but they will be memories that are important to you. You may want to repeat all or parts of this self-discovery exercise every couple years as a reminder of your uniqueness and value.

Find a serene and comfortable setting and begin appreciating the marvelous creation of *you* who was fearfully and won-derfully made by the masterful hands of God.

1. Think back to your childhood. Write about five or more of your memories, highlights, or activities that were especially meaningful, life-changing, or rewarding for you. After you have written about your memories, write about how you felt at the time.

2. Consider your adult years. Write about five or more of your memories, highlights, or activities that were especially mean-ingful, life-changing, or rewarding for you. After you have written about your memories, write about how you remem-ber feeling at the time (or how you think you may have felt).

3. What do you consider to be your greatest accomplishments? List or write about at least five.

4. What do you want to accomplish or complete during your lifetime? List or write about at least five.

5. Are you aware of natural gifts, strengths, skills or qualities that are part of who you are? These are talents that you didn't necessarily learn in school or from someone else.

6. Make a list of the ten most important interests in your life. Now rewrite them in order of priority.

7. How would you like to be living your life ten years from now? Think about your relationships, your work, your social involvement, your home, your financial picture, etc.

8. Take some time and write about your dreams. If you could do anything, and money was not an object, what would you do?

9. Are there people or projects that depend on you? List them (in order of priority as much as possible). It may be helpful to write your feelings about each of these responsibilities.

10. Now write anything about yourself that comes to mind. Keep it positive. This is not the time to write about your failures, your shortcomings or your weaknesses. Write about what you can do. Try to imagine the mind of God when he created you. What special things did he want for you and your life?

11. File all your work in your notebook under "Who I Am."

Don't worry if you can't answer all these questions right now. Getting to know who you are, what you want, and how you want to live your life is a process. We are now at the starting point of recording what you already know. This is your time of discovery. Relax. Let your image unfold. Trust the truth that you were intentionally created with a specific purpose for being.

An Unlikely Candidate

At first glance, Andrea Taylor's life looked doomed. She dropped out of her high school in rural Montana when she learned she was pregnant. She married and had two more children before her marriage fell apart. As a single mother of three, Andrea packed up her children and moved to Colorado where she landed a clerical job at a university. She decided to accept an offer to take college courses at the reduced tuition rate offered to employees. Andrea worked diligently, and finally, at age forty, she earned her degree. She remarried and moved with her new husband, his three children, and her three children to Seattle. It was here that Andrea realized the work God wanted her to do.

Even though Andrea had little experience teaching school, she believed God wanted her to make Christian education available to the youth others had cast away. She started Seattle Street School, an accredited high school where forty teens and young adults now come for academic and life lessons. Many of the kids are homeless, gang members and teen parents whose lives also seem doomed. But Andrea and her staff come alongside these kids to love them, teach them and help them change their lives.

On the outside, Andrea was an unlikely candidate. But God knew she was the right person on the inside and now she's living according to his purpose for her life and making a life-changing difference for others.

3

It's a Matter of Principles

*Life is like a can of sardines—we're all of
us looking for the key.*[1]
Alan Bennett

WHEN OUR FAMILY BEGAN OUR JOURNEY out of the rat race,
we didn't have travel agents or tour guides telling us where
to go or how to escape. We didn't know where to start and we
weren't even sure where we would end up!

First we focused on getting our financial picture in order. We
spent time figuring our net worth. We developed a plan to pay
off debt. And we put together a spending plan that aligned our
expenditures with what we considered to be our priorities.

I was on a personal retreat (I go away by myself a couple of
times each year to read, write, watch movies I've always wanted
to see, and still myself so I can think, pray, and hear God) when
I stumbled upon what I now believe is one of the most effective
first steps to take to get out of the rat race.

I started reading Stephen Covey's best-selling book, *The
Seven Habits of Highly Effective People.* Covey's message is
sound, current for today's problems and offers excellent guidance for anyone trying to make sense of their lives. Covey
believes the most effective people act according to time-proven
principles—principles such as fairness, kindness, dignity, respect,

charity, integrity, honesty, quality, service, patience, personal growth, and obedience to God.

On the surface, that sounds fairly simple. In fact, my first reaction was to think, *Oh, I'm already doing that.* But then I started examining my principles. I asked myself, "Just what do I believe about guidelines or standards for living?" The deeper I probed, the more I began to understand the value of identifying the principles by which I live and then purposefully reordering my life and my actions to reflect what I believe. Covey calls it principle-centered living. I call it *living from the inside out* or *intentional living.* Regardless of the title, defining and then living according to our deeply rooted principles is key to finding meaning and fulfillment.

Principles are boundaries, the natural laws of humankind. They are embedded in our souls as the primary guidelines for *right living.* They are the limits we endorse in order to live together as a civilization. Principles embody the rules for relationships. They are deep, fundamental truths that have universal

When you begin the work of defining and articulating your principles, from what source will you draw direction, insights, truth? I found the Letter to the Romans written by the apostle Paul around 57 A.D. to be an excellent source for compiling sound, time-proven principles for living. Biblical scholars consider Romans the primary and most excellent book in the New Testament. The letter is the most complete and detailed statement of the gospel and God's intentions for our lives. Paul uses the foundation found in the Old Testament to explain the teachings of Christ.

As I read each chapter, I began listing principles found in the text. When I finished reading Romans, I used my notes to write my principles for living. They were sound two thousand years ago and they are sound now.

application. Principles enable us to be members of sound and healthy families and growing, stable communities. While principles are not necessarily religious in their origin, they are written on our hearts by our Creator. They keep us moving onward and Godward.

Covey helped me understand that our effectiveness is predicated upon certain inviolate principles—natural laws in the human dimension that are just as real, just as unchanging as the law of gravity is in the physical dimension. These principles are woven into the fabric of every civilized society and constitute the roots of every family and institution that has endured and prospered. Throughout our lives, we have acted in certain ways because of our principles.

Principles for healthy and good living begin with who we are inside. As Ralph Waldo Emerson put it, "Though we travel the world over to find the beautiful, we must carry it within us, or we find it not."[2] That beauty is found by living according to those timeless, changeless truths written on our hearts.

Our principles are part of who we are. Living according to our principles develops rich character and depth in our personality and adds strength to our constitution. Our principles show us the way to security, confidence, and satisfaction. We can act out of who we are rather than in response to the ways we think others expect us to act. Our principles help define us, so if we want to truly know who we are, we must first gain a clear understanding about what we believe.

IDENTIFYING AND DEFINING OUR PRINCIPLES

Principles can be divided into two major categories: inward principles and outward principles. *Inward principles* are those that shape our character and bring us to health and wholeness:

courage   integrity   self-respect
faith   self-discipline   serenity
honesty   self-reliance

Outward principles govern or direct our actions in the world and our interactions with others. They are the outward expression of our inward beliefs:

charity   love   service

justice   loyalty   respect

kindness   obedience to God

When we hold tight to our principles and allow them to direct our actions, we choose a path that leads us into a life of meaning and significance.

LIVING FROM THE INSIDE OUT

I didn't realize it early in our relationship, but I see now that one of the qualities that first attracted me to my husband was that his life actions reflected his inner principles.

Fred comes from a long line of members in the Society of Friends (also known as Quakers) which was founded in England by George Fox. The Friends are against violence and war. Christ's command, "love your enemy," is taken literally and over the centuries the Friends have been involved in many peacemaking efforts. This belief has earned members of the Society of Friends the distinction of pacifists and peacemakers.

Fred's maternal Quaker roots can be traced to George Fox himself, who around 1665 led to faith Valentine Hollingsworth, the family patriarch. Hollingsworth migrated to the Colonies at the invitation of another Quaker, William Penn. We've also traced Fred's fraternal Quaker roots back to the late 1700s. Both Fred's grandmothers, Susie Shrauner and Cora Gregory, were Quaker ministers, as was his father, Dean Gregory.

While Fred held tight to his Quaker beliefs, he didn't sense a call to become a pastor. Instead, he pictured himself as a college administrator or dean (it's clear to all of us who know and love him that college administration was Fred's idea and certainly not God's plan for his life).

The Vietnam War raged on in 1966 as Fred approached graduation from George Fox College in Newberg, Oregon. While the war concerned him greatly, Fred knew he would never fight in Vietnam. His pacifist convictions, his Friends heritage, and his involvement with the church paved the way for Fred's qualification as a conscientious objector (C.O.). When he was eighteen years old and required to register for the draft, Fred sat before the Selective Service Board and was granted the status of C.O.

> "In matters of style, swim with the current; in matters of principle, stand like a rock."[3]
>
> **Thomas Jefferson**

Fred made plans to continue his education after finishing at George Fox College. He was registered to begin graduate studies at the University of Oregon. Everything seemed set. But Fred's designs were interrupted when the Selective Service Board removed graduate school deferments for those not enlisting in the armed forces. While Fred would not be forced to engage in war, he still was required to complete two years of alternative service.

The menu for alternative service was fairly broad as long as conscientious objectors volunteered at a registered non-profit service agency. Fred's choices included driving delivery trucks for the Salvation Army, working as an orderly in hospitals, and teaching underprivileged children and counseling troubled youth. Fred was considering these possibilities when his philosophy and religion professor, Arthur Roberts, addressed the students at an assembly. He more or less asked Fred and his classmates if they were willing to put their money where their mouths were—in other words, were they willing to be demonstrative about their anti-war belief and serve in Vietnam as peacemakers and caregivers?

Fred didn't actually go through the exercise of evaluating his principles and weighing them against the options. But he felt a deep stirring inside that said, "Go." He was acting from the inside out.

In the summer of 1966, Fred and two of his classmates, Jon Newkirk and Jerry Sandoz, left their comfortable and peaceful town of Newberg and journeyed to Vietnam where they worked for more than two years with a consortium called Vietnam Christian Service. Fred developed a feeding program for war-displaced persons. He organized and started a vocational training school for youth. Later he helped introduce a variety of high-yield rice to the tribal people in the mountains of central Vietnam.

Vietnam changed Fred's life. He felt a call on his life to serve the poor, displaced, and powerless people in our world. Fred's commitment to his principles and his willingness to let them define his actions led him into a life vocation of caring for those in need.

Living according to our principles doesn't always require us to make such dramatic life moves. Sometimes it's as simple as correcting a cashier's mistake who otherwise would give us more change than we are due, apologizing to a colleague if we make a mistake in judgment, or serving food at a homeless shelter. But there also are times when we encounter hurdles that cause us to wrestle with our beliefs. Living according to our principles isn't always easy. I know from personal experience.

A RESPECT FOR LIFE

I will never forget the evening when I received a call from our oldest daughter. "Mom, I went to the doctor today. I'm pregnant." Under other circumstances this would be joyful news. I love children and I looked forward to being a grandmother. Except I didn't want to be one so soon. Not now. Not when my daughter wasn't married.

Over the next several days, I spent a lot of time worrying, crying, writing, praying, and talking with my husband. I had to sort out my feelings and decide how I was going to handle this news. My daughter doesn't always take my advice, but she trusts my judgment and often comes to me for guidance. I knew I had to be very sure of what I told her.

Abortions are generally safe, quick, legal, and the option many women choose when faced with an unplanned pregnancy. On the surface it would be easier for my daughter to terminate her pregnancy and wait until she was prepared to care for another's life. But while it seemed the easier option, I couldn't bring myself to suggest an abortion. My reverence for life overpowered my desire for an easier solution. I couldn't advise an abortion—but I couldn't leave her hanging, either. Therefore my belief that all life is sacred called me to encourage her to carry the child growing inside of her. My convictions also called me to offer my caring support, my unconditional love, and my ongoing assistance. She took me up on my offer.

Today I am the grandmother of the cutest, smartest, and most precious little boy around. For some reason, he adores and cherishes his grandmother. He is my treasure and I can't imagine my life without him. Having a baby hasn't been easy for our daughter. She wasn't able to finish college, her social life is greatly curtailed, and she works two jobs so she can afford rent, food, clothing, and child care. Assisting her means that we baby-sit several times a week, and since she is single, we provide much of the support normally offered by a spouse. But the joy we receive from our grandson, the bond we share with our daughter, and the peace we feel about following our principles, far exceeds the extra effort we all expend.

Acting according to time-proven principles may not always be the *easiest* way to live—but it is always the *right* way to live.

A GIFT TO OUR CHILDREN

As Fred and I learned more about living from the inside out, we received an unexpected gift of self-confidence. We found that *knowing* our principles for living often freed us from confusion. Discovering our principles and then aiming our actions in their direction increased our knowledge about why we do what we do, why we believe what we believe. Knowing who you are and what you believe is the definition of self-confidence, and we wanted to pass on this gift to our children.

We realized we frequently addressed the *actions* of our sons rather than the *underlying causes* for their actions. We were trying to treat the shriveling leaves of the tree rather than trying to heal the diseased roots.

Linda and Richard Eyre, authors of *Teaching Your Children Values* and parents of nine children, consider the home the primary place for children to learn principles and values: "[Another parent's] value system may be very similar to—or it may differ from—ours. The important thing, we feel, is that parents consciously develop their own set of family values and work at teaching those values to their children. The home will never, should never, can never, be replaced as the institution where basic values are learned and taught."[4]

One Saturday morning, Fred and I joined each other with cups of coffee, paper, and pens in hand. We talked about each of our boys and tried to name their strengths and their weaknesses. Then we looked at the life principles we could connect with their actions. For example, our seventeen-year-old son Seth's strengths are self-confidence, a fun sense of humor, intelligence, creativity, and a passion for sports. On the other side, he rarely picks up after himself, his bedroom defies description, and he has trouble completing homework assignments.

Fred and I concluded that Seth needed to learn self-discipline. So we talked with him about our thoughts, gained his insights, and then all three of us worked out a plan: First, Seth set some goals about study time, physical exercise and money management. We decided to meet two times each week at neighborhood cafes and coffee shops to review his progress toward his goals and brainstorm about ideas for success. We set some guidelines for our own behavior—no judgment, only objective advice—and established that this is a work in progress. We didn't expect overnight change—but we all wanted constant movement forward. Seth also talked to an adult friend who gave him some helpful hints about asking for help sooner and recognizing the signs of procrastination. Seth began to understand more about himself and made a personal decision to change his behavior so he could achieve the results he wanted.

While we're still in the process of change with Seth, he's experiencing success. He gets up at 5:30 A.M. three days a week and runs. His savings account is growing. And slowly but surely, his grades are improving as he devotes more time to study and homework. Together we're attacking the root of the problem rather than merely nagging at the symptoms.

Dawit, on the other hand, is the most self-disciplined member of our family. I'd love to take credit, but he came to us that way, so our goal is to preserve rather than instill. Dawit's challenge is a lack of self-confidence in some areas. So again, Fred and I brainstormed and developed a plan to help Dawit gain more self-assurance. We decided to be very specific when we acknowledge Dawit's accomplishments and teach him about giving himself appropriate pats on the back. Instead of limiting our compliments to, "Good job on that essay," we say, "Dawit, you did a good job with your punctuation in your sentences. The way you tell the readers about how Anna felt when the Nazis came to her door helps them experience her fear. And you did a neat job in your penmanship. You must feel very proud of the good effort you put into this paper."

The Lord, and most of our friends, know our kids aren't perfect. Our lives are a building process and all of us are still under construction. But parenting using this perspective has given Fred and me a clearer vision to set goals and measure success. We're able to be very intentional about guidance, rewards, discipline and communication, and our sons are maturing into fine, happy young men with rich and sound characters. We're proud of them, for them, and with them.

DEVELOPING A RICH CHARACTER

If we study our nation's past we can see a gradual disintegration of the rich character that once personified our country. Covey offers an excellent explanation when he evaluates the *success literature* that began flooding the market more than fifty years ago.

It was filled with social image consciousness, techniques, and quick fixes—with social Band-Aids and aspirin that addressed acute problems and sometimes even appeared to solve them temporarily, but left the underlying chronic problems untouched to fester and resurface time and again.

In stark contrast, almost all the literature in the first one hundred fifty years or so focused on what could be called the Character Ethic as the foundation of success—things like integrity, humility, fidelity, temperance, courage, justice, patience, industry, simplicity, modesty, and the Golden Rule.... The Character Ethic taught that there are basic principles of effective living, and that people can only experience true success and enduring happiness as they learn and integrate these principles into their basic character."[5]

After World War I, the definition for success shifted from the Character Ethic to what Covey calls the Personality Ethic, where the measurement of success depends on one's personality, public image, attitudes and behaviors, and skills and techniques. The depth and quality of one's character has been relegated to a lower status. This is the very measurement used to determine today's American Dream. Even more damaging, it's the measurement used by our society to determine the value of you and me. This crazy-making system, where our public image gains us points on the success chart, is what got us into the rat race, and it's what keeps many of us there.

BACK TO BASICS

When interest rates soar or when the stock market plummets, wise investors wait for the correction. That is, they wait for the extraordinary conditions to return to a more normal or balanced state.

Similarly, the definition for success appears to be undergoing a "correction." We are beginning to see signs of change. The popularity of Covey's book

> "I am only one; but still I am one. I cannot do everything, but still I can do something; I will not refuse to do the something I can do."[6]
>
> **Helen Keller**

is one indication that people are looking for answers and that they are interested in returning to a principle-centered lifestyle.

When society's principles are taken away, destruction results. I believe that's what happened in the Soviet Union. Seventy years of Communism shredded the principles by which the people in that land lived. When Communism fell, Russian, Ukrainian, and other Baltic leaders quickly realized that the tenets of Communism had nearly obliterated the rich character once found in their people. They saw that the current generation and their children were void of sound principles.

After studying the problem and looking for possible solutions, Russian leaders decided the principles that serve as the foundation of Judeo-Christian belief were greatly needed in their society.[7]

They contacted hundreds of Christians from throughout the world to come to Russia and show the state-run schools how to teach students the Ten Commandments and the teachings of Christ. They didn't want their children evangelized, but they believed the principles taught in the Bible were fundamental. They wanted their children to learn them. The Russian leaders, in their quest to rebuild their nation, wanted teachers to tell students "thou shalt not murder, thou shalt not steal, thou shalt not commit adultery, thou shalt not lie." They wanted the next generation to grow up understanding that we should "love our neighbors as ourselves," that we "should not judge lest we be judged," that "it is more blessed to give than to receive."

Many of us grieve over the conditions of our American cities, the rise in violent crime throughout our nation, and the unstable world being inherited by our children. But thankfully, we have the remnant of sound principles from which to build. We may not, as individuals, be able to change the world. But we can change ourselves. We can choose to adopt sound principles and act in response to their guidelines. In doing so, we ignite another candle in the darkness and make new light for the world.

YOUR TURN

1. Identify ten life principles you want to live by (refer to the list of internal and external principles). Write each of the principles on the first line of a sheet of notebook paper. For example: honesty, human dignity, excellence, service, integrity.

2. Under each of the principles, write a definition. You may find using a dictionary helpful for this step. Example: "Honesty is the act of telling the truth."

3. On each of the pages, write the outcomes of the principle when it's exercised. Example: "When we are honest with people we gain their trust. We feel good about ourselves. We feel secure in our actions."

4. Now write at least three ways in which you can act according to each of your principles. These can either be actions

that you are already taking or actions you want to begin.

5. After you have finished writing about ten principles, add others that may come to mind. Write them on sheets of paper, add their definitions, their benefits and ways you can act upon them.

6. Add all these sheets to your notebook under "Who I Am." They will serve as the foundation for writing your mission statement.

Flexible for God

Drs. Paul and Margaret Brand are considered two of the leading authorities in their specialized fields of medicine. But, they're quick to admit, it wasn't because they planned it that way. "I wanted to be an engineer," says Paul, the notable hand surgeon. "I worked in construction and resisted any suggestion that I consider medical school. Thankfully, I followed God's plan for me rather than my own. I've learned that we must remain flexible if we are to fulfill his plans for our lives."

Margaret, an ophthalmologist, agrees. "I remember moving to India and telling the people with whom I would be working that I would do anything except eyes. I hadn't any training nor interest in the field. But then they told me they desperately needed a doctor to help patients with their eye problems and would I please consider it. I said I would, and haven't stopped yet."

The Brands, now retired from regular practice, spent many years working with victims of leprosy, pioneering treatments that have since revolutionized the care. They continue to address professional groups throughout the world... and keep a very flexible schedule!

4

Uncovering Your Life Equation

The world as we live in it, is like a shop window in which some mischievous person has got in overnight and shifted all the price labels round, so that the cheap things have high price labels on them and the really precious things are priced low[1]

William Temple

IN THE SNOWY JANUARY of 1991, Fred and I decided to go away for a week to spend some concentrated, uninterrupted time discussing our values, priorities, and goals. We packed the car with a few casual clothes, some books, our writing materials, and a couple of bags of groceries. After driving east over the Cascade Mountains and along the Columbia River, we arrived at Lake Chelan in north central Washington. We settled into a comfortable, lakefront condominium which would serve as our seven-day thinking, praying, dreaming, and planning sanctuary. We relaxed in the serene setting on the long, narrow lake, which lay between the mountains like a wide, winding river. We felt as if we had taken nature's tranquilizer. We slept deeply. We cleared our minds of worries and distractions. We opened ourselves to new thoughts and ideas about our future together.

During the first of couple days we talked, slept, and read. Then we started getting down to business. What kinds of experiences did we want in our lives? What were our priorities?

What gave us joy? What caused us concern or tension? What did we value? What made us feel valuable? What did we want to accomplish before we died?

Søren Kierkegaard said, "Life can only be understood backwards; however, it must be lived forwards."[2] As I look backward and consider our week at Lake Chelan, I now understand that it served as a very important change point in our life together. We took a necessary recess from the busyness of our lives to calm ourselves. We took a time-out to seek God, to think and to listen to ourselves and to that still, small voice in our souls.

During our retreat we captured on paper fleeting hopes and fading dreams so they couldn't get away. We wrote down the relationships and activities that were most important to us. We identified goals and wrote the framework for a plan for our lives for the next decade.

I now understand more clearly why artist Nicolas Poussin titled one of his paintings "A Dance to the Music of Time." Fred and I began learning steps to a new dance during that week. A new beat sounded in our hearts and a sense of freedom and joy began to saturate our souls. We started taking sure steps, moving in a harmonious dance to the music of time in our lives. Establishing our principles and then identifying our values laid a foundation for our future.

PRINCIPLES VS. VALUES

People frequently use the terms "principles" and "values" interchangeably. I prefer to distinguish them. *Principles* determine the perimeters for living. They provide the broad brush strokes for the way we choose to live; they are the foundation for a way of life. *Values*, on the other hand, are the specific building blocks we consider most important for our unique lives. Our *values* grow out of our *principles*.

I like to think of my principles as the boundary lines surrounding the immense, lush forest where I am afoot on my life journey. Many others travel the same forest because we follow the same principles, but the paths I choose to trek, or the trail map I follow, is charted by my values. Two people may share the same principles yet follow very different life paths because their values differ from one another.

For example, you and I might agree on the life principles "Love one another as you love yourself," and "Do unto others as you would have them do unto you." But the way we live out those principles is determined by our values. Since one of my core values is to serve the poor in developing countries, I give money to support self-help programs in countries such as Somalia, Vietnam, and Haiti. A core value for you may be to serve homeless women and their children in your community, which leads you to volunteer one night a week at a shelter.

Our life journeys ought to be an intentional response to the principles and values we hold dear. We can choose the direction we want to travel through life by clearly defining our values, then permitting them to serve as our compass.

During our week-long retreat, Fred and I contemplated our gifts, hopes, dreams, and what we believe to be truth. Our *principles* include:

- Love God with all your heart, all your mind, and all your soul
- Make love your aim
- Pursue truth
- Foster honesty, discipline, service, and health
- Respect and honor God's creation
- Seek justice, health, dignity, and respect for all people

We identified our priority values as:

- Our commitment to God
- Seeking health and wholeness as individuals
- A loving relationship as husband and wife

- Loving relationships with each of our children and our grandson
- Love and commitment with members of our extended family
- Positive, growing relationships with our friends
- Serving and advocating for the poor in our world
- Fostering a respect for all life, including other people, property and nature
- Being good stewards of our resources
- Seeking financial independence to allow more freedom to volunteer our service in the areas where we can address the greatest needs
- Demonstrating, through our actions, that every human being is a valued creation of God and therefore deserving of our compassion, care, love, and respect

Since that time the circumstances of our lives have changed, and we've gained a clearer understanding regarding some issues. But for the most part, the discoveries we made that week about our lives, our priorities and our values, have stayed intact. We were able to get in touch with who we were, with what we wanted, and with how we wanted to live our lives.

While many of us may share the same life principles, we will differ in our values (or at least in the rank and order of our values). This is where we begin seeing the reflection of our unique individuality, gifts, talents, dreams, desires, responsibilities, and circumstances. It's also where we start to see our society and its effect on us.

Over the course of the last few decades, our society's principles and values have tilted in directions many of us recognize as off-balance. "Do unto others as you would have them do unto you," has been exchanged for, "what's in it for me?" The values of hard work and integrity have been overshadowed by a desire to get rich quickly. The needs of children have been usurped by the greedy desires of adults.

As William Temple observed, "the cheap things have high price tags on them and the really precious things are priced low."[3] Most of us know men and women like Megan who scramble for wealth, image, and power, even while their important relationships suffer and disintegrate. Designer clothes, cars, and homes have become more significant than excellence, charity, and humility. The pursuit of riches has superseded

> "It's not hard to make decisions when you know what your values are."[4]
>
> **Roy Disney**

the pursuit of true happiness. The trivialization of religious devotion has replaced the hunger to know and serve God. Slick movers and shakers are often popular and powerful, whereas intelligent, focused people are considered nerds.

Inevitably, the consequences of our out-of-balance lifestyle are catching up with us. We're looking at the paths we've chosen to follow and we're saying, "I want out of that rat race. Show me another way... and hurry!"

Identifying your values is an important step in designing your personal route to escape the rat race. While we share many common values, the importance you place on specific values won't be exactly the same as mine, your friends' or your neighbors'. We are unique. We have varied responsibilities. We have different gifts and desires. These distinctions are revealed in our values.

Our values may change as we travel through various stages of our journey. Young people may hold education, career development, and friendships as high values. Single adults may choose a cause or a vocational track among their values. Men and women who appreciate creativity may select art, music, and literature. Husbands and wives may place being a good marriage partner and parent on their lists.

Here is a list of words to spark your thinking about those

values you believe to be important:

art	education	independence
beauty	environment	interdependence
charity	family	joy
children	financial freedom	justice
church	friends	leaving a legacy
communication	fulfillment	literature
community	health	marriage
creativity	home	music
cultures	parenting	philanthropy
religion	social issues	travel
wealth	work	

After identifying those values that are most important to us, yet another step is critical to making sure we keep first things first.

IT'S JUST ONE THING

One of the cable movie companies cast its lure into our television room by offering a weekend of free movies. So one evening, even though I had seen it before, I cuddled up under a quilt and watched *City Slickers*, starring Billy Crystal and Jack Palance. It's the story of three harried businessmen escaping New York City for a couple weeks by joining a cattle drive from New Mexico to Colorado.

I was again struck with the relationship between the tough-skinned cowboy named Curly (played by Palance) and the city slicker named Mitch (played by Crystal). After a rough and tumble beginning, Curly allowed Mitch into his private inner world. Riding on their horses through the rough terrain, Mitch sensed a peace and contentment in Curly's being. "What's your secret to life, Curly?" Mitch asked.

Curly smirked then chuckled lightly, "Your types spend

about fifty weeks a year getting knots in your rope. Then you think two weeks up here [driving cattle] will untie them for you. None of you get it."

Then, holding up the index finger of his gloved hand, Curly offered Mitch a precious, gleaming pearl of wisdom: "It's just one thing. You stick to that and everything else don't mean [dirt]."

Mitch asked inquisitively, "Well, what's the one thing?"

With a look of confidence, Curly said, "That's what you figure out."

It took Curly dying on the trail and Mitch nearly drowning as he and his other city slicker pals drove hundreds of cattle across the plains, down the valley, and through the rivers—but Mitch found his *one thing*. The discovery changed his life. Even though he returned to the busy city, his active family, and a job he didn't like, Mitch had taken the first step to getting out of the rat race. He had identified what he valued most in life.

The *one thing* for Mitch was his family. His brush with death stripped away the illusions that clouded his vision. He now recognized that his wife and his two children were the most important parts of his life. He wanted to be a good husband and a good father. His family and the significant part he played in their lives was his number one priority... his *one thing*.

REAL-LIFE CITY SLICKERS

Many of us real-life city slickers are finding our *one thing*, too. My good friends Rich and Karmann Kaplan (I call them my "guinea pig friends" because I test a lot of my ideas on them) discovered their *one thing* several years ago. Both were busy professionals, zipping from one project to the other. Like most baby boomers, they spent more money than they earned and often searched for fulfillment in exciting experiences and impressive possessions. Their best time, energy, and resources were centered on their work, travel, and accumulating desirable objects.

All that changed in 1986 when Rich and Karmann confronted a major crisis. As they put it, "We got hit with the reality-pie-in-the-face." Karmann was seven months pregnant with their first child when she started feeling contractions. The doctors tried everything possible to delay the birth. As a precaution, they took tests to determine the maturity of the infant's lungs and determined they were developed enough for survival. When Karmann lost so much amniotic fluid that her baby's health was jeopardized, the doctor ordered an emergency Caesarean section.

Meanwhile, Rich had flown to San Francisco to attend a large conference. Sitting in the meeting hall, he was surprised to look up and read on the presentation screen, RICHARD KAPLAN REPORT TO THE INFORMATION DESK IMMEDIATELY. After learning of Karmann's hospitalization, Rich headed directly for the airport and caught the first available flight back to Seattle. He arrived at the hospital just before they rolled Karmann into surgery.

The surgery was a success and Matthew entered the world weighing four pounds, three ounces. But the doctors were concerned. Matthew's breathing was irregular. Not wanting to take any chances, the doctor ordered the newborn to be transported to Children's Hospital where he could receive the emergency neonatal care he needed. Rich climbed into the ambulance and traveled the ten or so miles with his tiny, hour-old newborn. "Never in my life have I felt so out of control," Rich told me several years later. "I couldn't do anything to fix the situation. That was the first time I prayed desperately. I pleaded with God to save my son's life."

Matthew received excellent care at the hospital and survived. Today he is a healthy, thriving, and active child. While Rich and Karmann wouldn't wish a similar experience on anyone, they treasure the priceless lessons they learned in those desperate hours.

"What's really important becomes incredibly clear when you face a crisis like we did," remembers Karmann. "We realized that night that living at a fast pace, climbing the corporate ladder, and accumulating things couldn't hold a candle to this precious life that we almost lost."

A couple years later, Lauren was born. Today, Rich and Karmann's family is the center of both their lives. Karmann quit her job and now stays home so she can give more attention to the children. Instead of writing business plans,

> "We realized that night that living at a fast pace, climbing the corporate ladder, and accumulating things couldn't hold a candle to this precious life that we almost lost."

she kneads Playdough and mixes finger paints. She helps run the cooperative preschool where Lauren attends and she also volunteers at the neighborhood elementary school where Matthew is enrolled. Karmann manages and implements the multitude of details found in homes today. She frequently relieves other moms who need a helping hand, a baby-sitter or a taxi driver. Several days a week, she also offers her friendship to me while we sip lattés, plan get-togethers, discuss our children, share parenting techniques, and consider ways we can improve our lives.

Meanwhile, Rich enjoys his work at Microsoft as a manager and technical evangelist (he travels throughout the country informing business people of cutting-edge software applications). While he is loyal to his employer and challenged by his work, Rich still accepts or rejects career opportunities after *first* considering the impact his decision will have on his ability to be home with his family, supportive of his wife, available to his children, and not consumed by job-related stress and pressure.

Of course, it's not necessary to wait for a reality-pie-in-the-face to realize the genuine priorities in our lives. Instead, we can go to a beach, a park, or some other quiet getaway. We can reflect on our lives and uncover what is most important to us. We can determine our personal *one thing*... and define our own values.

When we make these discoveries, and center our lives and our activities around them, we can begin living intentionally. We can find meaning in our lives and we can begin making a positive difference in the lives of others. Defining your values is an essential step toward living a fulfilled and enriched life.

WHAT MAKES YOU FEEL WORTHWHILE?

Part of uncovering our life equation is determining what makes us feel worthwhile—what makes us feel valued or valuable. For example, I feel valuable as a mother to our children and as a grandmother to our grandson. I know the greatest gift I can give each one of them is unconditional love. My unique and intimate connection to their lives leaves a forever imprint on their souls. We all understand that I'm the parent and they are the children, but we are also playmates, friends, and partners. I offer my assistance to help them become the best they can be; I try to keep an open-heart policy; and I hope to communicate to them that they are treasured. As I see my children growing in self-esteem, responsibility, confidence, and joy, I feel valued because of the positive influence I may have had along the way.

I also feel valuable as a creative person. I love taking an artistic approach in every task or project I assume, whether it be cooking, writing, making gifts, gardening, teaching, or designing. When I create something that looks beautiful, that changes lives for the good, or that gives pleasure—I feel valuable.

Involvement in activities that are important to us gives us fulfillment. But who tells us when we're doing OK? Who passes judgment?

WHO IS YOUR JUDGE?

During some rough times in my life, I picked up a book called *Joy That Lasts*[5] by Gary Smalley. The thesis of the book is that most of us look outside of ourselves for a measurement of our value or worth. We rely on *people, possessions, places,* and *position* to tell us we're OK, that we're making it. Consequently, we *dress for success.* We *climb the corporate ladder.* We *fight for a title* on our business cards. We *buy impressive cars and fancy houses.* In doing this we allow people, whose values we may not even agree with, to be our judges! We let them pass judgment on our personhood or determine the worth of our contribution.

Because we want to impress our judges, we keep giving more of ourselves so we can build and maintain an image they will like. We work harder to make more money so we can spend more dollars to climb the mountain of material success. We get crushed if someone criticizes our attire. Kids tease other kids who aren't wearing the *right* brand of jeans, and some adolescents even kill so they can have a pair of sport shoes with the *right* logo on the side.[6]

We measure our worth by our position in life. We feel devalued if we're *just a secretary.* Women who choose to stay home with their children often feel diminished in professional gatherings. We consider men and women to be successful and significant if they hold numerous academic degrees or are the CEO of a business—even though they may be cheating on their spouse or not giving their children the time they need and deserve. Yet, we hold these people as our models to establish and measure our standard of living.

I'm sure you respect many men and women. You may know a few who are especially righteous. But do you know anyone before whom you would be willing to stand so they could pass judgment on you? My guess is, probably not. Even if you know of someone who could meet the standards of a judge of character, they likely have enough integrity and wisdom to know they are not worthy to cast their verdict on you or on anyone else.

Those of us in the rat race aren't the only ones who accept the judgment of frail humans. Read these heartfelt words from a monk: "I know that I have often let worry about work disturb time set aside for prayer and reading. Public prayer time is also invaded by anxiety about work, and often I spend an entire [service] thinking about what I need to do as soon as I leave

---

If we are to discover the unique person God created us to be, we must have the time for exploring our souls. Listening to our hearts requires that we separate ourselves from the rush of the world around us. It is during these periods of separation—in our times of quiet solitude—that we can learn more of who we are.

Rarely will quiet time just happen. Rather, we must plan for it, free our schedules, and intentionally arrange for it. Here are some ways you might consider to find quiet time for your life:

1. Go for a long walk ending up at a cafe where you can think, write, and pray.

2. Get up early each morning for a week; read passages from an inspirational book and then write about your feelings, thoughts, and how you can act upon what you are learning.

3. Take a personal retreat. Arrange to stay in a cozy setting where you can rest, think, write, read, and listen. Check out reflection houses and contemplative centers often available to individuals and operated by religious orders.

4. Schedule a weekly date with yourself. Go to a quiet, comfortable cafe or coffee house where you can read, think, and explore yourself within.

the church. It is good to try to please others by the excellence of what we do to serve them. Unfortunately, I often forget the ones I am serving and let my own pride take over. In the desire to protect my frail ego, I worry about what others will think about my 'product,' whether I am working in the kitchen or the garden, or on a shopping trip in town. It's true that often it feels better to hear someone say that I did a good job than to see my lowliness in the light of the Lord, as often happens in prayer. I know that God loves me in spite of my lowliness, and someday I will learn to live by that knowledge."[7]

The reality is that there is only One who has the authority and the credibility to judge us. He is also the One who created us. He's the One who said, "Come to me, all of you who are heavy burdened [from trying to live up to the world's standards] and I will refresh you. I will give you rest [from your scramble for success]. For my burden is easy [just love me] and my yoke is light [because I am your Creator and friend and I want the very best for you]."[8]

God is our judge. Not people. When we shape our lives to impress him, we will find the inner peace and joy for which we long.

We all have memories of people treating us unkindly or hurting us in some way. Let us use the remembrance of that pain to serve as a tool to make us more sensitive to the impact we have on those around us.

SHOWING OTHERS THEY ARE OF VALUE

More than ten years ago, I took a class with several friends from my church. We used a study guide by Bruce Larson and Keith Miller called *The Edge of Adventure*.[9] One directive in the book has greatly impacted my interaction with people, especially children, ever since: "Other than family members, describe what you felt because of the person in your life who first made you feel valuable."

We were to give our answers to the class, not telling the person's name, occupation, or other information about them. Rather, we were to describe that person's actions and then explain how their actions made us feel.

I flipped through the pages of my memory. I finally stopped when I reached the chapter about my early youth in Ocean Park, Washington, a small town on the Pacific coast where my family lived for several years. We had a small house, kitty-corner from the elementary school where my father was a fifth-grade teacher.

Those were the days when women always wore hats and gloves to church, when doctors carried big black bags and made house calls, when butchers stood on sawdust-covered floors, and when uniformed men delivered milk, bread and clean laundry to homes.

One day when I was about four years old, the milkman came to our door and warmly greeted me as he dropped off our dairy order. I asked him if he needed any help delivering milk to our neighbors. Although I don't recall, I'm sure he gained my mother's approval before enthusiastically responding with, "Sure, come on with me."

He took my little hand in his, picked up his milk carrier in the other, and we climbed into his big milk truck with a black-and-white Holstein cow painted on the side. He lifted me up and sat me on the shiny metal box covering the truck's engine. Then he started driving the truck up the street toward our neighbor's house. I remember how odd it seemed that he drove standing up.

I helped load the milk carrier with bottles of fresh milk. Then he took my hand as we walked to the neighbor's kitchen door to drop off the order. We got back into the truck and headed toward the next house.

We must have delivered milk to five or six more homes on our block, then he took me back to my own house, thanked me for the help and said, "See you tomorrow, helper."

Of course, I was thrilled. What an adventure! For many

more months I delivered milk with our milkman, and every day I felt just as thrilled and helpful as the first.

I think it's telling that back in the '50s, a small-town milkman took a few minutes out of his day to make a curly-haired, round-faced four-year-old girl feel needed, useful, important, and valuable. Then, more than thirty years later, she was sitting in a class and feeling very moved by the memory of his simple, yet very important gesture. I don't remember his name or the color of the truck or the name of the milk company. But I can vividly remember how wonderful this kind-hearted man made me feel.

That classroom exercise made me understand the impact our actions can have on those around us. Our simple, unadorned gestures can imprint the heart of a child and bring joy and pleasure for years to come.

A big part of getting out of the rat race is bringing meaningful, healthy relationships back into our lives. Caring for others, as we want to be cared for, gives us balance, fulfillment and health.

If you find yourself feeling overwhelmed with all there is to do, consider forming this new habit suggested in *Finding Time* by Paula Peisner.[10]

"Always ask yourself three questions:

Am I beginning the most important things first?

How urgent is this task?

How can I get somebody else to do the task for me?

YOUR TURN

In your notebook, you've started to list your gifts, your heart's desires, and your principles. Now you will begin merging this information and start designing your road map for living by defining and prioritizing your values.

1. Using as many sheets of notebook paper as you need, title

each page with the values that are most important to you.

2. Compare each of the values you've written on your sheets with the life principles you identified in chapter three. Under the heading for each value, write a few notes about how the value integrates with your principles. For example, Andrea Taylor and Raven Johnson place a high priority on their value of helping youth at risk. Their life principles of treating people with respect and dignity shape the types of programs they develop for those they want to help. A priority value for me is financial security. My life principle of honesty keeps me from robbing a bank. My principle to foster health keeps me from working sixty-hour weeks.

3. On each sheet, list some ways you can act out your commitment to the specific value. For example, "I will help create a home where members feel loved, nurtured, and accepted." Or, "I will volunteer to tutor youth at risk." Or, "I will live within my financial means by following a spending and saving plan."

4. Now file your value sheets in your notebook under "Who I Am" *in the order of their priority in your life.*

5. On another sheet of paper, write your personal definition of success. Be as specific as possible. Is your definition of success consistent with your life principles and your values? For example: "I will be successful when I'm involved in activities to improve the human condition; when I'm following the teachings of Christ; and when I regularly sense peace and contentment in my everyday life." A definition of success for a period of your life may be: "I will be successful when I am free from all debt; when I have enough income to meet my simple needs; when I have completed my graduate studies; and when I am a full-time volunteer at the school for homeless children."

6. On another sheet of paper, list those activities or objects that make you feel valued or valuable. Consider the people or activities that affirm you and who you are.

7. Now list the people, or types of people, whom you have allowed to judge you, even if it's just in your mind. It might be parents, coworkers, society, spouse, church members. You may also want to specifically name people such as a parent whose standards you feel you must meet.

8. Finally, write a brief description of yourself. Who are you? What do you want? How do you want to live your life? This is your time to think about what can be.

9. File all your sheets in your notebook under "Who I Am" for later reference.

Organizing Tips

1. **Keep like things together** such as sporting equipment, medicines, sewing tools, books, holiday decorations, business papers, stationery, cleaning products.

2. **Designate places** in your home for specific activities. For example, designate a place where umbrellas, school books, mail, messages, keys, glasses, or laundry *always* go. Designate a place to eat, a place for projects, a place to clean shoes, a place to play.

3. **Make lists** of things you need to do, purchases you need to make, places you need to go, and people you want to see. Writing down our thoughts and ideas not only frees us from having to remember, but the practice also brings clarity and order to our intentions.

4. **Schedule** check-ups for your annual physical exam; visits to specialists; and reviews with your financial advisor, accountant, or tax attorney. Schedule maintenance appointments for your heating system, tree trimmers, chimney cleaners, window washers, and car mechanics. Schedule far in advance for vacations, flight plans, holiday visits, and performing arts tickets.

5

Writing Your Personal Mission Statement

*It concerns us to know the purposes we seek in life,
for then, like archers aiming at a definite mark, we
shall be more likely to attain what we want.*

Aristotle

I WISH WE HAD A DOLLAR for every lost dream. We could probably pay off the national debt and still have stacks of money left over.

Countless people meet their death never realizing what they could have accomplished in life. We're travelers on a long road. If we do the work to find our way and just keep moving ahead, we'll find at the end of our journey a wonderland like we have never imagined.

Instead, many of us get distracted by sideshows and carnivals along the way. We end up standing too long at the gaming booths, tossing rings in hopes we'll win the big, rhinestone-studded prize. We may get disenchanted and move to a carousel and mount a brightly painted horse only to find ourselves going in circles. Several times, we may return to the road and even enjoy our journey for a while. But then we are lured by the detours, those little side streets that keep taking us off the very track that will lead us to joy, fulfillment and meaning. All along, we really wanted the wonderland, but the glitter and the lights and the shouts from the carnival venders kept getting our attention.

Lost dreams. Lost hopes. Lost opportunities.

We do have choices. We can realize our dreams. We can intentionally shape our lives so that we do what truly gives us joy and fulfillment.

As we wandered and bumbled our way out of the rat race, Fred and I decided one of our primary goals was to live intentionally. We wanted to take charge of our lives and achieve what we felt called to do. We needed to discover our life purpose, our reason for being, our direction.

OUR DISCOVERY

We started thinking, remembering, and writing about our gifts, skills, desires and characteristics. We looked back over our lives, including our childhood years, and considered the activities that brought us the greatest sense of accomplishment and pleasure. Patterns started to emerge and soon we were able to define what we believed to be our purpose in life.

Tapping into the wisdom and experience of successful business practices, we decided to develop a personal mission statement for both of us as well as for our family.

Peter Drucker, Stephen Covey, Tom Peters, and other business gurus agree: an articulate mission statement is critical for successful enterprise. A mission statement expresses in words the purpose of a business or, in our case, the purpose of our lives. The mission of the Girl Scouts of the U.S.A. is *to help girls grow into proud, self-confident, and self-respecting young women*. The mission of a hospital emergency room is *to give assurance to the afflicted*. The mission of the Salvation Army is *to make citizens out of the rejected*.

According to Stephen Covey, a personal mission statement or creed "focuses on what you want to be (character) and to do (contributions and achievements) and on the values or principles upon which being and doing are based."[1]

I often tell people that their mission statement defines their who, what, and how: *who* they are, *what* they want, and *how* they want to live their lives.

Before we engage in the process of writing out mission statements, let's define a few words we will use.

Our *purpose* in life is forever and divinely ordained. Our purpose is unchanging and never completely finished. It's the foundation under the rest of our lives or an umbrella covering it. To be in perfect harmony with ourselves, everything we do should flow from our unique purpose.

Our *mission statement* articulates in one or more sentences our purpose in life. It states our purpose. Because we are all different, our mission statements will reflect the unique beings we were created to be.

Our *goals* are temporary. They take into account our current circumstances and responsibilities. They are tasks we start and finish. Our goals enable us to fulfill our purpose as defined in our mission statement. In most cases, several goals are required to fulfill one part of a single mission.

Our *actions* are the steps we take to achieve our goals. We may take several actions to achieve one goal.

Example: The Girl Scouts' **mission** is *to help girls grow into proud, self-confident, and self-respecting young women.* To fulfill their mission, they have many specific goals. One of the **goals** is *to fund the Girl Scout programs.* They achieve this goal by completing several **actions** including *selling Girl Scout cookies, collecting dues,* and *receiving foundation grants.*

The same sound practices implemented for successful businesses can be adapted for our lives. By discovering our life purpose and capturing it in a personal mission statement, we take a significant step in understanding who we are. When we know who we are, we gain confidence for what we are to do.

Our mission statement can act as our guide through life. As we move through the discovery process, we will understand more clearly the words of Aristotle when he said, "It concerns us to know the purposes we seek in life, for then, like archers aiming at a definite mark, we shall be more likely to attain what we want."

Perhaps one of the most famous mission statements is found in the First Amendment to the Constitution of the United States, known as the Bill of Rights:

> We, the people of the United States, in order to form a more perfect union, establish justice, insure domestic tranquillity, provide for the common defense, promote the general welfare, and secure the blessings of liberty to ourselves and our posterity, do ordain and establish this Constitution of the United States of America.

Francis of Assisi's familiar prayer reads very much like a mission statement:

> Lord, make me an instrument of your peace. Where there is hatred, let me sow love; where there is injury, pardon; where there is doubt, faith; where there is despair, hope; where there is darkness, light; and where there is sadness, joy. Grant that I may not so much seek to be consoled as to console; to be understood as to understand; to be loved as to love; for it is in giving that we receive; it is in pardoning that we are pardoned; and it is in dying that we are born to eternal life.

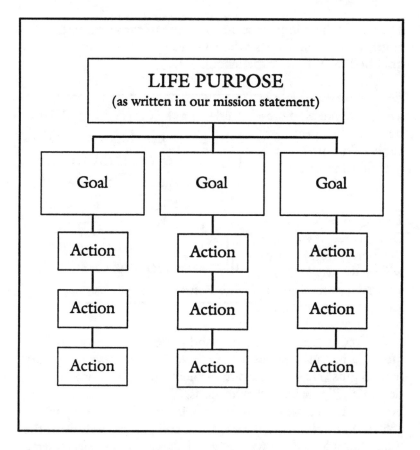

DEVELOPING A PERSONAL MISSION STATEMENT

Remember, our personal mission statement articulates our purpose in life. There are three elements to consider when discovering the purpose for which we were specifically and uniquely created:

Look at your gifts, talents, and dreams. When we peel away the masks and costumes that can hide the real us, we begin to see a person with an imprinted heart. Some of those imprints were engraved on our hearts when God created us. Others were inscribed by our past experiences.

Look at the needs of our world. We are all members of humankind, each of us born at a specific time to fulfill a need.

Look at our principles. Our principles define the perimeters within which we work. They also fuel our engines and give us commitment, drive, and enthusiasm.

"My task is to simplify and then go deeper, making a commitment to what remains. That's what I've been after. To care and polish what remains till it glows and comes alive from loving care."[2]

Sue Bender

As Fred delved into his past and present and considered his future hopes and dreams, he was able to target several primary natural gifts. He's been aware of them since his earliest memories. His gifts make him who he is. They define his character, his uniqueness, his personality. He is kind and helpful; adaptable and flexible; tenderhearted and compassionate toward the weak; humble and approachable. His greatest desire is to serve God by loving the individuals with whom he has relationships and by caring for people in need.

After identifying these traits, Fred recalled an Old Testament verse that seemed to capture his gifts and characteristics. He adopted the verse as his mission statement:

[Your Father] has showed you, O man, what is good; and what does the Lord require of you but to do justice, and to love kindness, and to walk humbly with your God?

Micah 6:8

One of the ways Fred fulfills his mission is through his work at World Concern, a Third World relief and development agency. As the executive director, Fred's focus is to mobilize, guide, encourage, and support members of the staff as they work together to develop self-help programs in some of the poorest and most remote villages in our world. He advocates for the poor and encourages men and women of means to share and invest their resources in World Concern's initiatives. Fred also defends those individuals whose voices are lost in the noise of the more powerful. He tries to show others that the poor and disenfranchised are worthy of dignity and deserving of hope.

It can be challenging to develop a family mission statement when half the members are very young. Mick and Drindy Fleming solved the problem this way. They started family meetings with their two young daughters when the girls were six and four years old. Mick and Drindy revised the idea of writing a family mission statement with developing family rules everyone agreed to follow. After talking about the subject several times in their family meetings, this is the list they developed:

Fleming Family Rules

1. Treat others like you want to be treated.
2. Always try to do your best.
3. Be honest.
4. Use your words—not your body.
5. Choose healthy food to eat.
6. Be respectful of other people's things.
7. Pick up after yourself.
8. Be true to yourself.

Soon after our friends Howard and Edith Berry married, they also chose a verse to give a clear direction and purpose for their lives together: "As for me and my house, we shall serve the Lord" (Jos 24:15). They clung to that verse through the twenty years of their marriage while they served the poor in Africa, raised three wonderful children, and were treasured friends to many. When Edie died in 1990, we all knew she had lived a life in her wonderland. To the very hour of her fatal heart attack, Edie remained on the path. While we miss her, we feel at peace because her purpose was fulfilled and our lives were enriched by hers. Meanwhile Howard continues on, being the father to his children, working on behalf of the poor, and being our treasured friend as he fulfills his call to "serve the Lord."

As I considered my past, I realized I also had a tendency to rally toward the underdog. I am tenderhearted and seek to understand others and their pain. I am joyful, celebrative, and creative. I find great pleasure when I am a channel for other people's joy. I believe we are called to love one another, and only when we can love perfectly are we worthy to judge (in other words—never judge others). My greatest desire is to know and trust God so deeply that I give him pleasure and I in turn enjoy a constant state of peace.

My personal mission statement says:

I will try to live my life according to the teachings of Christ; I will seek truth, health, joy, and respect for myself and for those in my care. I will exercise those habits of prayer, work, sleep, study, physical exercise, eating, and creating which I believe God has shown me to be right. I will serve the poor in body, mind, and spirit; and I will behave in ways that reflect what I believe to be truth.

Fred and I found our personal mission statements so helpful that we decided to develop one for our family. We called a family meeting and talked over the idea with our sons who still lived at home. After explaining the process and showing them our mission statements, we asked them to brainstorm with us about the importance of a family—even more specifically, our family. As individuals we all wanted mutual respect; we believed each person should work to become the best he or she could be; that self-respect and self-discipline were important values; and that habits of prayer, meditation, study, and service should be fostered and practiced. We all wanted a home that was safe, nurturing, and calm; we wanted our home to be a place where our friends felt comfortable and loved; we wanted to honor God and follow Christ's teachings; we wanted to be happy, joyful, and excited about life.

Our family mission statement reads like this:

Our home will be a comfortable, clean, and orderly living environment where our family, friends, and guests find joy, comfort, peace, happiness, and respect. We will seek truth and health and exercise wisdom in what we choose to read, see, and do at home. We especially want to love, learn, and laugh together and help and support each member of our family as they strengthen and use their unique gifts and talents.

We will do what we can to ensure that every person has access to adequate food, shelter, health care, education, and an opportunity to become all God intends them to be. We will do what we can to promote justice, security, and hope for all.

We will make every effort to be self-disciplined and self-starters, taking personal responsibility for fulfilling our unique purpose in life. We will act when appropriate and react when necessary.

We will try to be faithful in those habits of prayer, work, study, physical exercise, eating, and sleep which we believe God has shown us to be right.

We will become financially independent, seeking an

enriched life rather than riches. We will exercise wise stewardship by spending less than we earn, with our wants subject to our needs and means. We will use what resources and talents we have to improve the quality of life for those in need by sharing of ourselves and in turn enrich our lives and spirits.

Our mission statements serve as touchstones for how we are to live. Committing our life purpose to the words in a mission statement calls us to sort out and choose our priorities. It brings us to the inner places in our lives where we can read the message our Creator has written on our hearts.

YOUR TURN

1. Review the information you've already learned about yourself. Read through your worksheets and make notes about what you believe your mission to be.

2. Begin a list of statements that reflect your purpose.

3. Write your first draft of your personal mission statement.

4. File all this information in your notebook under "Who I Am."

5. When you are satisfied with your mission statement, copy it so that you can refer to it frequently. You may want to have it copied so it can be framed and hung in your living room or carried in your wallet.

6

How Much Is Enough?

We poor humans boast of our freedom, then exhibit our shackles of material enslavement. We insist that nobody can tell us what to do — but the clanking of our chains gives our plight away.[1]

Ralph Larson

OUR PURPOSE IS AN *INWARD* REALITY that results in an *outward* lifestyle. Up to this point, we have centered on our inner selves. We're now going to shift as we use what we've learned to help us determine how we will act. These actions include the way we relate to people, the work we choose, the leisure activities we favor, and the resources we consume.

JUST BE HAPPY WITH WHAT YOU'VE GOT

I grew up in the Seattle area with my parents, two sisters, and a brother. We lived in a "Wonder Years" kind of neighborhood of track houses where the families all knew each other and the kids were friends. My sisters and I were the only girls on our block, so playing often included flag football, pulling homemade hydroplanes behind our bicycles, Monopoly, and other games the neighborhood boys liked.

Mattel's Barbie hit the market when I was about eight years old, quickly passing Betsy Wetsy in a little girl's popularity contest for the favorite doll. The neighborhood boys weren't into girlie-type games, so I spent countless hours playing house and dolls with my sisters, Cathy, Jean, and Nancy.

We shared several dolls, a small suitcase filled with doll clothes and blankets, a small wooden cradle, a glass tea set, and several settings of doll-sized plastic dishes. We each established our own fantasy homes, trading dolls, clothes, and dishes along the way. Every once in a while, we would want the same doll or the same outfit. We would negotiate and try to be fair. But there were times when one of us may have felt slighted. That was the time when someone usually called an end to the negotiations by saying, "Just be happy with what you've got."

Plan for Fun

What activities are life-giving to you? What can you do for encouragement and fulfillment? Intentionally have fun by making plans today.

1. The arts: Are there museums and galleries you want to visit, plays and concerts you want to attend, book or poetry readings you want to hear? Call or write to the groups and organizations in your area that offer presentations and ask for their annual calendars. Make plans with your spouse or with friends. Purchase a season pass or tickets to those events you want to attend. Write them on your calendar now!

2. Make new friends and keep the old: Can you set aside the first Friday of each month to host a dinner party with friends? How about a movie or a picnic? Make a list of those friends you want to see, and make plans. Write them in your calendar now, including when you will invite them and what you will do.

At the time I didn't realize the wisdom in our phrase. But now that I'm an adult trying to make sense of my life in a consumer-oriented society, I appreciate the truth of our youthful insight.

Americans' obsession with accumulation, wealth, and power, along with our conditioning to want more, has made the concept of *enough* an archaic one. When do we have *enough* money? When is our job good *enough*? When is our house big *enough*? When is our car good *enough*? When do we have *enough* clothes?

The accumulation of wealth, the desire for more, the climb to the top—they're all part of an American agenda preached in the '70s, perfected in the '80s, and now questioned in the '90s.

3. Realize your dream: Do you have a dream vacation? Do you long to see the pyramids, the Vatican, the Wailing Wall? Planning ahead can turn your dream into a reality. Even if you need to save for five years—is that so long to realize a lifetime dream? Begin a savings plan, and in the meantime attend lectures, read books, study the language of the place you will visit.

4. Keeping in touch: Do you have out-of-town family members or friends who would love to hear from you? Can you buy or make some stationery and greeting cards and schedule one hour each week for letter writing?

5. Simple pleasures: Write a list of at least ten things you can do that give you pleasure. Do you long for private time? How about planning a day away to read at the beach? Do you have an interest not shared by other members of your family? Plan to do it by yourself or with a friend. Be good to yourself!

We're making more money than ever. Yet in these higher income times, the life savings of the average fifty-year-old is only $2,300.

Alexander Solzhenitsyn, who suffered many years in Soviet prisons, felt compassion and despair for those caught in the clutches of consumerism. He said, "The constant desire to have still more things and a still better life and the struggle to obtain them imprints many Western faces with worry and even depression, though it is customary to conceal such feelings."[2]

> "When the soul is troubled, lonely and darkened, then it turns easily to the outer comfort and to the empty enjoyment of the world."[4]
>
> **St. Francis of Assisi**

Wanting better, higher, bigger, and more keeps us searching. As Ivan Illich, an Austrian socialist, claimed: "In a consumer society there are inevitably two kinds of slaves: the prisoners of addiction and the prisoners of envy."[3] Continuing in a "make more, spend more" mentality keeps us in the rat race. We lose sight of our heart's real desires. We set ourselves up for failure or at best never feeling content. Our constant struggle to grasp the golden ring keeps us chasing an illusion rather than true meaning, happiness, and satisfaction.

THE DILEMMA

We make fun of and laugh about Imelda Marcos and her obsession for shoes. After all, how can one woman wear twenty thousand pairs of shoes in a lifetime? As our Jewish friends would say, "Enough, already!"

But when we think of the "make more, spend more" attitude so prevalent in our society, we may have to question our own appetite for accumulation. Does a pet rock make any more sense than Imelda's shoes? How about the Home Shopping Network? Or the philosophy, when I get bored I shop?

Visit a shopping mall on a Saturday afternoon and you'll see a perfect example of America's insatiable desire for more. Shoppers race from store to store, many carrying bags bulging with things they don't need. As one woman confided, "I often head for the mall without any idea of what I might buy. It's like entertainment. I even feel a rush when I buy things that are pretty. I know deep down that I'm not shopping for the items, but rather for the feeling."

If this woman were talking about a bar instead of a mall and about vodka instead of clothes or jewelry, we'd wonder if she were an addict. Psychologists are learning that for some, shopping and accumulating unnecessary things is an addiction.

PERSONAL CHECK-UP

Review your spending by looking at the previous three months in your check register. Divide the expenditures into the following categories:

1. Good buying decision, aligned with my values.
2. Why did I buy that?
3. I can't even remember this purchase.
4. That was a mistake!

Now go back and think of ways you can alter your spending habits so that more of your expenditures are in the #1 category, rather than in numbers 2, 3, or 4.

We will not find satisfaction until we identify what is *enough*. Without *enough* we will continue to spend beyond our means. Without *enough* we will diminish our ability to realize our dreams and to fulfill our purpose in life.

Americans have struggled with this for years. In the '50s, the measurement of success for men was based primarily on two criteria. One, their ability to be breadwinner; and two, their proficiency at disciplining their children. If a man's children stayed out of trouble and if he earned a large salary, he was deemed a success.

While many men aptly filled their defined roles, their sons and daughters sensed an emptiness by not having a positive relationship with their dads. When these boys entered adulthood and became fathers, a few more criteria were added: be a nurturing, loving father to your children and a supportive partner to your wife.

Add these expectations to our inflated lifestyles. Some of us paid more for the last car we purchased than we did for the first house we bought. The cost of living has soared. We want to travel *more* often and *further* distances. We want *more* expensive cars and *bigger* homes. We want *more* expensive clothes and *more* "things" for our children. We're working harder and putting in more hours to maintain *a new standard of living* which others continue to define for us. America has a new middle-class lifestyle of more and better which leaves many men, women, and even children, feeling deprived if they don't *have it all*.

We've created a breeding ground for failure. People enter a vicious cycle by taking on huge debt to feel and appear successful.

THE WAY OUT

Just to remind you, the definition of *enough: adequate for the want or need; sufficient for the purpose or to satisfy desire.*

Determining how much is enough helps establish boundaries, limits, and benchmarks. Defining *enough* enables us to develop a structure, an intentional plan for our lives. Wrestling with the concept of enough allows us to integrate our principles and values with our consumption and activity so we can accomplish our goals.

We halt the crazy-making cycle when we limit ourselves to *enough*. To say with conviction, "I don't need that," gives us a sense of confidence. Determining our own needs and their levels, rather than following the formula pushed by our consumer society, empowers us. Our definition of success is just that— *our definition*. It's based on sound principles that we believe to be true and that have stood the test of time. It's based on the values we each consider to be most important to us. It's a reflection of who we are, what we want, and how we want to live our lives.

Because of our uniqueness, what is enough for me may not be enough for you. We each have different hopes, dreams, values, and goals, and we therefore can afford to give one another the flexibility to determine our own needs.

SHOPPING IN THE '90s

As I mentioned in the first chapter, when Fred and I decided to harness our disheveled financial matters, we scrutinized our spending and kept track, down to the penny, of each expenditure. I soon learned I spent a lot of money on things that didn't align with my values and with what I wanted from life. I faced the fact that my *buying philosophy* was, "If I like it, I buy it."

I didn't like that part of my character. I had always thought of myself as more controlled and well-intentioned. It was a bitter pill to swallow. But uncovering this truth about my spending habits served as a springboard, encouraging me to form healthier shopping practices. In some cases we decided to cut back, and in others we chose to spend more. I learned to buy clothes according to need and purchase only replacement kitchen items (previously those were two areas where my spending was out of balance with my values).

On the other hand, Fred and I like doing things with each of our children and we're especially active with our two sons who still live at home. All of us enjoy sporting events. So we spend what others may consider to be an exorbitant amount on tickets to watch Seattle's pro teams, the Sonics, Mariners, and Seahawks.

Defining your spending philosophy, adjusting it according to your values and definition of *enough,* and then aligning your purchases with your priorities are all important steps for your escape from the rat race.

Before you make a purchase, think about what it is you are actually buying. Consider its value and its part in your bigger plan. Is making this purchase taking you closer or further from your long-term goal?

WHAT'S YOUR PHILOSOPHY?

Here are some of the areas to consider as you determine how much is enough for you:

House: What qualities do you want in a home? Is ownership important? How about size? Location? Style? Status? How do you use your home now? Is it a place of retreat and solitude? Do you entertain? Is your home a place of comfort and relaxation for your benefit, or do you consider it a badge or trophy for others to see? Does the home you live in now or the home of your dreams match your values? What is enough for you?

During one of your quiet times, consider your personal ties to material goods. What things are attached to your ego? When would you feel embarrassed in relation to things (either having them or not having them)? What things do you use to define who you are to others?

After you've made up your lists, think of ways you can change your thinking process and your behavior to reflect your values and beliefs.

Car: My friends Rich and Karmann Kaplan used to drive two expensive cars: a silver Volvo station wagon and a black BMW. Their car payments totaled more than their monthly house payment. They decided to keep the Volvo since it was a safe, quality car for their family with two small children. But Rich decided his BMW was more than enough for him. He sold it and paid cash for a used car. His new-to-him car is comfortable, serviceable and (listen to the sweet ring of these words) *paid for!* What changes do you need to make to align your mode of transportation with your values? When is your vehicle good enough?

Clothing: What emotions are linked to the clothes you buy? Do you go in debt to buy ensembles so people will think you're successful, intelligent, or wealthy? Take a look in your closets and drawers. Do you have more clothes than you need? Do you ever go to the mall to look for something—anything—to buy rather than for a specific purpose? Do your clothes give you value?

Entertainment: How often do you go out? How often do you invite guests to your home? How much do you spend each month on entertainment? At one point, our family was so busy we almost installed a revolving door! We finally determined that two evenings away from home per family member per week was enough. If one of us needed to go beyond that limit, we checked in with the rest of the family. We also have friends in our home quite often. Several times each year, Fred and I make a list of people we want to entertain. Sometimes that turns into a small dinner party; other times it's a picnic or a simple dessert. By being more intentional about our comings and our goings, we're able to maintain and develop those relationships that are important to us within reasonable time and financial limits.

Debt: Asking if you have enough debt is a little ludicrous. But how about too much? My favorite financial advisor, Jane Bryant Quinn, has a formula to help you determine how much debt you can safely carry. You can find it on page 128 in chapter nine.

We've determined that any debt is too much for us, so part of our plan is to be debt-free in eight more years. That means we're not incurring any new loans and we're paying off current debt as quickly as we can.

Dining: Do you go out to eat so often that it's not a treat anymore? How about the dinner bills? How much do they add up to each month? It's not uncommon for a family of four to spend more than $300 a month at restaurants. Some families even spend more at restaurants than they do at the grocery store.

We seldom eat out any more. Instead we work on preparing special dinners at home, and several times a week we dine by candlelight with linen napkins and flowers. When we do go out to dinner, it's for a special occasion and we all appreciate it much more than we did before!

Furnishings: Do you need a Street of Dreams house to feel fulfilled and happy? Or will cozy couches with stuffed cushions suit your style? Do you spend a lot of time at home so you're willing to invest in good quality furniture and art to make it especially comfortable? What is enough?

Gifts: When you buy a gift, what are you really purchasing? A special item that expresses your love and care for the recipient? Or are you trying to buy their love and approval? Does your tree get buried by all the gifts surrounding it on Christmas morning? How many gifts are enough? When have you spent enough on gifts?

Home Improvements: Fred and I delayed remodeling our kitchen because we couldn't afford the $20,000 contractors told us it would cost. We put up with ugly wallpaper and a dingy appearance for more than seven years. Finally we got the "aha" and decided a total remodel was more than we needed. Changing the wallpaper, replacing the sink and countertops, and installing new curtains would be enough to meet our needs. We did some of the work ourselves and the total bill came to under $1,000. Our kitchen may not be featured in *Better Homes and Gardens*, but it's just right and *enough* for us.

Household Items: Is clutter a problem in your home? Are your drawers and closets bursting with things you don't even use? Is your attic, basement or garage packed? As George Carlin reminds us, we have a lot of stuff.

The difference between clutter and enough often results in hours of time. Fewer items mean we don't lose, dust, or shuffle and store as many things. As we off-load what we don't need, we often find a new sense of peace and order in our lives and emotions.

> "We will not find satisfaction until we identify what is enough. Without enough we will continue to spend beyond our means. Without enough we will diminish our ability to realize our dreams and to fulfill our purpose in life."

Money: Here's the biggie. When do you earn enough money to live a comfortable, meaningful life? Do you earn enough now? Could you reduce your workload and be happy with much less? Would living on much less actually make you happier? Points to ponder, friends.

Travel: Do you need to travel to all corners of the world to feel complete? How about concentrating on Scandinavia, Mexico, Canada, or the British Isles?

Do you venture out enough? Maybe you could open a world of discovery by saving toward a photo safari in Kenya. How about using your skills in a refugee camp in Africa?

Vacations: Most members of the rat race don't take enough time *off!* How much and what kind of a vacation do you need to feel refreshed and relaxed? Can you plan vacations that are restful, or are you one of those who needs to get back to work to return to a reasonable pace?

Work: Okay, here's another difficult area. When is your job good enough? Do you need to keep climbing that corporate ladder? Do you have an end in sight? When have you put in enough hours? When is your title good enough? When are the standards of performance you set for yourself and for others high enough? How would your spouse, friends, and coworkers describe your relationship with your work? Does the amount of time, energy, and commitment you give to your work match your priorities and values? Check it out. You may be surprised.

It's important to keep in mind that we're all different. We have various needs, circumstances, passions, desires. What is enough for you may not be enough for me. Perhaps I can go completely without in an area you consider essential. It's important to go through the steps to learn who you are so you can better understand what you want and when you hit that freeing level of *enough*.

YOUR TURN

In the past several chapters, you've investigated your life purpose, defined your principles, examined your values, and started to write your personal mission statement. All of these exercises help bring our desires into perspective—into the perspective of who we are.

Taking into consideration all you have learned up to this point, complete the following exercises:

1. On a blank sheet of notebook paper, begin writing what you consider to be *enough for you* in the following areas (add others that may relate specifically to your interests and activities):

Car	House
Clothing	Household Items
Debt	Improvements
Dining	Toys (children and adults)

Education	Travel
Entertainment	Vacations
Furniture	Work
Gifts	

2. In what areas do you believe you have too much (write or rewrite your list and put them in priority order)?

3. What actions can you take to curb your appetite for more? What can you do to begin shifting your desires away from more and closer to *enough*?

4. What three actions can you begin immediately which would help you feel more balanced and more in control of your consumption and activities?

5. File all your sheets under "What I Want."

7

Here I Am

Before you can plan where you want to go, you need to know where you presently are.

Anonymous

Fred has worked in international development since the mid '60s. He has focused on extremely poor villages where 40 to 50 percent of the children die before reaching their first birthday. His efforts are centered on designing self-help programs for the people such as developing better farming techniques, improving diet and hygiene, expanding education programs, and creating income-producing cooperatives. The overall objective is to design programs that empower the residents to raise their health and economic conditions to such a level that they and their children can become self-sufficient, productive, adult citizens.

The very first step in designing a program is to conduct a *baseline study*. In other words, Fred must first know where people are before he can design a program to move them to a new level. He must know the *current conditions* before he can determine what must be *changed*.

Those of us who want to escape the rat race must do the same thing.

While our stakes aren't life and death (feel blessed because you probably live better than 80 percent of the world's population), we know that the way we're living isn't what we want and that we want to change. But before we can design our program to travel in a different direction, we need to know where we are. Our baseline study requires us to gather data that will answer the following questions:

1. To what and to whom am I responsible?
2. What time is it on my life clock?
3. What is my financial condition?
4. What earning power do I possess?
5. What areas do I have the ability to change?

TO WHAT AND TO WHOM ARE YOU RESPONSIBLE?

Relationships and commitments bind us together as families and communities. They impact our lives, our actions, and our decisions. Some are subject to choice and change. Others are not. For example, you may want to quit the job to which you have a commitment, but you can't quit being the child of your parents, the partner of your spouse, or the parent of your child.

I am responsible to God, myself, my husband, my children, and my grandson. I believe I should "do unto others as I would have them do unto me." My family members' actions affect me and my actions affect them. I want to consider them in the goals I set and the decisions I make.

I also have commitments I want to maintain during this time in my life. I work with several non-profit organizations which depend on me as a consultant. I want to publish the monthly newsletter, *Out of the Rat Race.* I want to serve the poor. I want to be an active member of our community. I want to participate in my church community.

Identifying our key relationships and our chosen commitments gives us vital pieces of data necessary to develop our life plan and our specific goals.

Taking Care of Business

A re there some things you can do to relieve pressure and stress in your life? Invest time and financial resources now for continuing dividends in your future.

1. *Savings for a rainy day:* Do you feel financially secure? Would you feel better if you had some money set aside for an emergency? Arrange to have a specific amount deducted from your paycheck or your bank account each month. Purchase savings bonds or invest them in another safe and secure plan. Every financially secure person started somewhere!

2. *Home improvements:* Would organizing your closet, fixing that broken knob in the bathroom, or replacing your washing machine make your life easier? Prepare a master list of those big and little jobs that need to be done around the house. Then one by one, get them done!

3. *Do unto others:* List at least ten things you can do to "make someone happy" (I love Jimmy Durante's version of that sweet song). Think of your family members, friends, coworkers. Send a card with encouraging words. Deliver flowers for no special occasion. Practice doing those random acts of kindness.

4. *Let bygones be bygones:* What clutter can you get rid of? Can you target one type of item that you can toss, recycle, sell, or give away? Old clothes, files, books, sporting equipment, housewares?

5. *Skeletons in the closet:* Are there some issues that a counselor could help you clear up? Do you have a nagging memory or painful attitude that needs healing? Find new freedom by claiming victory over the problem.

WHAT TIME IS IT ON YOUR LIFE CLOCK?

We also have some reality checks to consider. One of them is age.

The old saying, "Don't put off until tomorrow what you can do today," gained greater meaning for me when Fred and I started looking at our goals and identified those dreams we wanted to realize in our lifetimes. It happened during our week at Lake Chelan.

At the time I was forty years old and Fred was forty-six. I actually love being my age. I've learned so much through my life experiences, and I realize maturity is a valuable gift we earn through our successes and failures. On the other hand, I have many years ahead of me, and I look forward to my future and all it holds.

One of the dreams Fred and I share is to offer our skills to empower the poor by volunteering with World Concern or another agency working in the Third World. To do that, we want to be debt-free and financially independent (which does not mean affluent) so we can give of ourselves without requiring a salary.

While we discussed the possibility, I said to Fred, "It would be great if we could reach our goal of financial independence in ten years." His reaction was sobering, but it also helped us shape our goals to meet our reality (you can read about our work toward financial independence in chapter one).

"I'd like to do that a lot sooner," Fred said. "I'll be fifty-six years old in ten years. My dad died when he was fifty-two. Most of my other relatives died in their early fifties. I don't want to work at an occupation all my life and die before I realize some of my important dreams."

Fred was saying, "I don't want to put off until tomorrow what I can do today. I may not see that tomorrow."

Obviously, we're not acquiescing to the notion of an early death for Fred. On the other hand, as we look at our life plan, we need to consider the reality of our genes and our health.

Acknowledging that reality caused us to advance our date for volunteering full-time. It also causes us to give more attention to our physical and spiritual health.

Fred and I merged our lives when we developed the following clock for our life as a couple. It's also good to develop a clock as an individual. The large numbers represent our ages. The titles within the pie pieces describe our major activities during those years of our life. The R&R doesn't necessarily mean we'll be totally retired (or dead for that matter), but we're not prepared to make plans for those years, at least not yet. Check in with us around 2015.

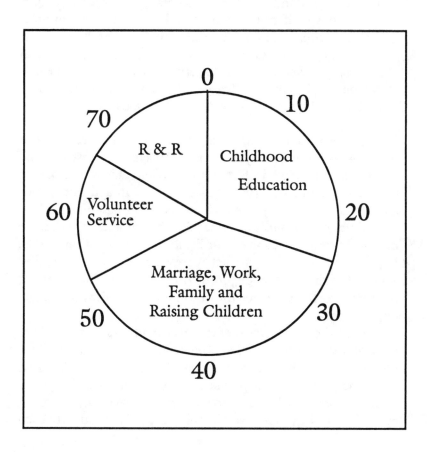

WHAT IS YOUR FINANCIAL CONDITION?

Like it or not, money does make the world go 'round—at least in a sense. Earning a living requires a disproportionate chunk of our time, as Joe Dominguez and Vicki Robin point out in their best-selling book, *Your Money or Your Life*:

Most of us spend much more than forty hours out of the week's total 168 hours earning money. We must take time to dress for our jobs, commute to our jobs, think about our jobs at work, and at home, "decompress" from our jobs. We must spend our evenings and weekends in mindless "escape entertainment" in order to "recreate" from our jobs. We must occasionally "vacate" from our jobs, or spend time at the doctor's office to repair our job-stressed health. We need to plan our "careers," attend job seminars or union meetings, lobby or picket for our jobs.[1]

With the amount of time, energy and emotion we invest in our jobs to make money, it's wise to make the most of what we acquire—that we in fact *earn a living*. This is just one of the many reasons why our financial net worth and our spending habits are such important elements in our base-line study.

Our net worth is like our financial bottom line. It's what we have after we subtract all of our liabilities from all of our assets. It is to be hoped that our net worth increases as we age and approach retirement. Sadly, most Americans are clueless about their net worth and enter the autumn of their lives financially unprepared.

One of the best investments I ever made was my purchase of *Making the Most of Your Money*[2] by Jane Bryant Quinn. Quinn's approach to personal financial management is based on sound principles, her points are easy to understand, the text is fun to read, and you'll find a good answer to just about every financial question you'll ever have. My frequently-used copy is a valuable resource in our library.

Knowing our current *specific* spending habits gives us the information we need to know if we want to cut back or redirect our expenditures. I emphasize *specific* because many people think they know how they spend their money. They're usually the same people who moan, "Where does it all go?"

Do a quick computation yourself. Add up your annual expenses—rent or mortgage, food, clothing, insurance, car, etc. Now add up your annual income minus tax. Subtract your total expenses from your total income to find out how much money you should have sitting in a bank account somewhere. Are you asking the question, "Where did it all go?"

We often don't do things that are important to us or engage in activities we really like because we feel as if we can't afford the expense. But we can realize many of the goals we thought we couldn't afford by being more intentional about our spending and redirecting dollars to align with our values and purpose.

But we must first know *what is* before we can prescribe *what to change*.

WHAT EARNING POWER DO YOU POSSESS?

Because our lives must be financed, we also need to consider our earning power. For example, thirty-seven-year-old Beth, a graphic artist, decided she wanted to be mortgage-free by the time she celebrated her forty-fifth birthday. That meant she needed to increase her annual income by $5,000. Some of that would be realized through pay increases at work, since they were more than cost-of-living raises. But Beth still needed approximately $3,500 more dollars each year. She realized she could clear about $25 an hour as a free-lance graphic artist. That meant she needed to generate one hundred forty hours of free-lance work each year to meet her goal. She was able to do that by landing a contract to lay out a company's monthly newsletter. Beth applied all the proceeds from her free-lance work to paying extra principal on her mortgage.

When Fred and I were developing our goals, we tried to estimate the amount of money we could earn each year. Fred's earning power was fairly easy to figure because he's salaried and we know the kinds of raises the organization gives. My earning power has more flexibility because I'm an independent consultant. The more billable hours I work, the more money I make. We've made a decision to increase my work hours so I can bring home more dollars that will go to debt reduction.

To determine your earning power, write down what you now make per hour or each month. If you are currently unemployed, what would be a reasonable level of pay for the skills you have now? Do you have restrictions about the number of hours you want to work? Are there some classes you can take or some experiences you can gain that will increase your employment value?

Determining your earning power gives you a valuable piece of information necessary for planning your financial future.

WHAT AREAS DO YOU HAVE THE ABILITY TO CHANGE?

The final pieces of data for our baseline study involve boundaries and limits. Our individual circumstances prevent us from making some changes—or at least we can't change right now. For example, mothers of pre-schoolers often want to wait until their children start elementary school before returning to work. Perhaps you are a single parent and can't quit your job and go to school full-time. If you are single, you likely have sole responsibility for some financial obligations that set boundaries for you. On the other hand, we have tremendous opportunities for change in most areas of our life. When we identify the areas we can change, we're able to design goals that will lead us to success. We can change, at least to some

Money: How to Give It Away

Many good causes need and deserve our support. To make your contributions the most effective, select a few good works and support them generously, rather than giving small amounts to several organizations. By generously supporting a few organizations:

- a smaller percentage of your giving will be used on raising funds from you

- you'll know when to say YES and when to say NO when you receive fund-raising appeals

- you'll be able to learn more about the organization and the work they're trying to accomplish

- you'll be a bigger drop in their bucket!

Before you donate to an organization, check out its reliability with the Better Business Bureau (BBB) in its headquarters city. Also, write or call the National Charities Information Bureau (NCIB, 19 Union Square West, 6th Floor, New York, NY 10003-3395, [212] 929-6300). NCIB will provide you with a summary of three different organizations. By meeting the standards of these two watchdog organizations, you can be assured your dollars are being used properly.

Think about the needs in your community, state, nation, and world. What concerns pull your heartstrings? What services do you consider the most important? What organizations can best deliver service to meet the needs?

Generously supporting the services provided by sound organizations is a way we can "give back" some of the blessings we've received. It's a good and right thing to do... and as you give more of your resources away to improve people's lives, you will learn through experience that it truly is more blessed to give than receive.

degree, the way we use our time and money. Many of us can change where we live, what we drive, who we entertain, where we volunteer, what we do for fun, how we learn, and what we plan for our future.

Reinhold Niebuhr's famous Prayer for Serenity notes that there are many aspects about our life that we do not control. If we acknowledge this reality and accept the "cards that are dealt us," we can maintain a healthy outlook and issue healthy responses:

> God, grant me the serenity to accept the things I cannot change, the courage to change the things I can, and the wisdom to know the difference. Living one day at a time, enjoying one moment at a time; accepting hardship as a pathway to peace; taking, as Jesus did, this sinful world as it is, not as I would have it; trusting that you will make all things right if I surrender to your will; so that I may be reasonably happy in this life and supremely happy with you forever in the next. Amen.[3]

YOUR TURN

The following questions, charts, and tools will help you gather the necessary information for your personal baseline study. Make sure you date each page, as this data provides valuable information that establishes your history. From the results of this baseline study, you will be able to measure your progress in the future.

1. On a blank sheet of notebook paper, list to what and to whom you are responsible. Include family relationships, religious beliefs, and professional commitments.

2. On a blank sheet of notebook paper, draw a large clock, replacing the minute number with decades of life (see sample on page 97). Record the time already passed on your per-

sonal time clock. Consider your family health history to provide a sense of the *hour*.

3. On a blank sheet of paper (even better if you can use a computer spreadsheet of a money management program such as
Excel, Lotus, Manage Your Money or Quicken) develop a
Net Worth Worksheet that suits your particular situation.
Use the one below as a model. Determine your current net
worth—be as exact and realistic as possible and make sure to
date and save your work.

QUICK ASSETS

Amount

Cash in checking, savings and money market accounts ..._____

Other mutual funds.._____

Stocks, bonds, government securities, unit trusts..........._____

Publicly traded partnerships......................................_____

Other easily salable investments................................_____

Money owed to you from work you've completed ...._____

Life insurance cash values ...._____

Precious metals..._____

Easily salable personal property: jewelry, silver, cars ...._____

Sub-total: ...._____

RESTRICTED ASSETS

Amount

CD's, if they have early withdrawal penalties..............._____

Retirement accounts: IRAs, Keoghs, tax-deferred
annuities, company thrift accounts, deferred salary .._____

Current worth of your vested pension, if payable
in a lump sum..._____

Executive stock options ...._____

Sub-total: ...._____

SLOW ASSETS

	Amount
Your home	_____
Other real estate	_____
Art and antiques	_____
Other valuable property: furs, boats, tools, stamps, coins, etc.	_____
Restricted stock, not readily salable	_____
Money owed you in the future	_____
Equity value of your business	_____
Sub-total:	_____
TOTAL FOR ALL ASSETS	_____

LIABILITIES

	Amount	Int. Rate
Current bills outstanding: this month's rent, utilities, medical bills, insurance premiums, etc.	_____	_____
Credit card debt	_____	_____
Installment and auto loans (current balance)	_____	_____
Life insurance loans (if you're currently paying them off)	_____	_____
Home mortgage	_____	_____
Home equity loan	_____	_____
Other mortgages	_____	_____
Student loans	_____	_____
Loans against investments, including your margin loans	_____	_____

Other loans   _____   _____

Income and real-estate taxes due   _____   _____

Taxes due on your investments
    if you cash them in   _____   _____

Taxes and penalties due on your
    retirement accounts if you cash
    them in   _____   _____

TOTAL LIABILITIES   _____   _____

NET WORTH (total assets minus total liabilities)   _____

4. Determine your spending habits by keeping detailed records for at least one month. On a sheet of paper (best to use a spreadsheet tablet or a computer), list all your monthly bills and their actual amounts. Categorize them using the list below (add categories if necessary):

Savings	Auto insurance
Mortgage/rent	Auto loan
Heat/light/water	Credit card companies
Telephone	Back bills
Life insurance	School/college
Health insurance	Child care/support
Disability insurance	Groceries
Homeowner's insurance	Clothing
Doctor/dentist	Housecleaning
Veterinarian	Personal care
Gasoline	Laundry
Bus/subway/taxi/ferry	Contributions
Restaurants	Furniture
Entertainment	Birthdays/holidays
Sports/pastimes	Vacations
Books/magazines	Pocket money
Repairs/upkeep	

5. Purchase a small spiral or stitched notebook that you can carry in your purse or pocket. Record every expenditure, including the amount, the place, and the category (see list above). At the end of the month, total the amount you spent by category and add these amounts to the sheet you started in the previous step.

6. How much do you make at your current job? Do you have potential to earn more? How many more years can you work for an income? Do you have the ability to earn extra income? Write the answers to these questions on a sheet of blank paper.

7. Consider the areas of your life you can change now or in the near future. Write a list of options such as debt reduction, profession, location, income, work situation, etc.

8. File all this information in your notebook under "Facts of Life."

8

Get a Grip

*Who of you by worrying can add
a single hour to your life?*

Matthew 6:27

A report by the Public Health Service indicates that our stressful lifestyle is linked to the six leading causes of death–heart disease, cancer, lung ailments, accidents, cirrhosis of the liver, and suicide. The medical community's study serves as a warning that our *life in the fast lane, the rat race,* the *way we live*–is actually becoming the way we die!

Research indicates up to 75 percent of visits to primary care physicians are for stress-related complaints.[1] The list of ailments from health professionals includes anxiety, asthma, chest pains, dizziness, exhaustion, headaches, high blood pressure, hypertension, infertility, migraines, muscle rigidity, peptic ulcers, rapid heartbeat, skin disorders, and excess sweating. Mental health professionals say suicide attempts, nervous breakdowns, and violent behavior all can be stress-related.

It's clear that we need to change our hazardous lifestyles. If we value life and want to be part of it for as long as possible, we must choose a lifestyle that fosters health, wholeness, and longevity. We've got to get a grip.

Experts contend that stress soars when people sense a loss of control, a loss of choice, and unpredictability. Conquering stress requires an internal commitment to principles and values, an ability to embrace life stresses as challenges, and a sense of inner control.

We can acquire all three of these stress-reducing needs by developing clearly defined goals and plans that are products of our purpose, principles, and values. But first we must face the fact that....

WE CAN'T DO IT ALL

When I interview subscribers to the newsletter or give a workshop, I often hear "I'm so busy." Yet, when asked about their accomplishments of the previous year, most people are hard-pressed to recall any one achievement they considered significant.

"When I think about it, I get up, hustle around the house so I can get to work on time," a banker told me. "Then I come home, down some dinner, plop in front of the television, then drop into bed... just to repeat the same routine the next day."

The struggle of coordinating family, social, and business demands seems to overwhelm both men and women. "My husband and I both work outside our home," recounted one working mom. "So we have to coordinate our schedules and tasks, including shopping, preparing meals, dropping off and picking up our children, and running household errands. Our two children are still pretty young and need our attention. So even if I've had a busy day, I still want to give them a lot of caring time.

"It's hard, and I have to say our busy schedules have had a negative effect on our marriage and on our friendships. My husband and I don't have time to visit with each other. Most of our conversations are more like strategy meetings to make sure all our work gets done. I can't remember the last time we had a meaningful get-together with any of our friends. I think most of them have gone on without us. We're just too busy right now."

Mick and Drindy Fleming own a child care facility in Seattle's downtown business center. Mick told me some busy parents have gotten so overwhelmed with their daily details that they actually forget to pick up their children. "It usually happens when the parents' normal routine changes—like the father is out of town on business, so the mom needs to fill in and pick up the kids," he explained. "Not

> "If we value life and want to be part of it for as long as possible, we must choose a lifestyle that fosters health, wholeness and longevity. We've got to get a grip."

long ago, I got a frantic call from a father who lives on Bainbridge Island [a suburb of Seattle reached by riding a ferry for thirty-five minutes across Puget Sound]. He had boarded the ferry and was visiting with several other commuters on their way home from work when all of a sudden he remembered he was supposed to pick up his son from our child care center. He rode the ferry all the way to the Island, rushed to the terminal to call me, then rode all the way back to Seattle. I waited for him and he finally arrived around 7:30. He was real embarrassed."

Most people find themselves in a reckless juggling act so they can complete all they have committed to do. Co-ordinating children's activities, parent meetings, church and social commitments—and then just normal living requirements—are stretching and stress-producing. "I hate to admit this," winced the mother of four who is currently separated from her husband, "but the other day I was really tired, and I felt completely overwhelmed with all that I had to do. I lost control of my emotions and just screamed at my kids and told them I didn't want to be a mother anymore.

"I would do anything to retract those awful words," she said, fighting back the tears. "I really hurt my kids and realized the horror immediately. I spent the next couple hours reassuring them of my love and that I would never leave them. I pray they'll forget the incident, but I'm afraid they won't."

Angry outbursts aren't the only negative result of trying to do too much. Physical symptoms are also common. Anxiety spells which mimic heart attacks are on the rise. More and more adults suffer from insomnia, high blood pressure, and ulcers. Long-term stress can result in serious ailments. New studies show that we may be increasing our chances of cancer because of our stress-ridden lifestyles.

Another woman, who seemed to tiptoe into the minefield of working women's issues, said, "I shudder to admit it, but I now realize I can't do it all. In the '70s and '80s, we were told we can have everything... women can have great careers, meaningful relationships, a wonderful family, and an active social life. But you know, now that I'm forty-something, I'm not so sure.

"Don't get me wrong, I'm not saying women aren't capable. And there certainly is more room for growth when it comes to women's rights and equality issues. But what I believe now is that the do-it-all or the have-it-all expectation is impossible. Impossible for everyone—male or female. I'm not so sure men or women can meet the incredible challenges in the professional world and also be the nurturing, caring spouse and parent we want to be at home."

Even monks, who are known for living simple and serene lives, are experiencing stressful changes. Brother Abraham, a monk at the Episcopal church's St. Gregory's Abbey in Three Rivers, Michigan writes:

A paradox of our culture is that even though the need for monasteries is growing as our society continues to disintegrate, our monasteries are becoming more and more like the world around them—a world to which monasteries are supposed to be an alternative. One important area in which monasteries are becoming like the prevailing culture is the increasing amount of time and effort given to work. More and more people are so tired from their workload that God means less and less to them simply because the time and energy to build a friendship with God does not exist in their lives. This unfortunate pattern is even becoming apparent in monasteries. Monks are supposed to lead a balanced life of work and prayer (and leisure), but our society's problem of overwork has invaded and influenced our monasteries."[3]

But there is a way out of the messy mire of busyness.

YOU CAN'T DO IT ALL, BUT WHAT CAN YOU DO?

I spent several years advising non-profit organizations about their marketing and fund-raising efforts. Commonly, there was much more to be done than there were budget or employee hours. To help my clients work through their priorities, I would ask, "You know you can't do it all right now, but what can you do?" Answering this question helped the leaders and managers establish their priorities, take first steps on what would eventually become full programs, and move them closer to accomplishing their long-term goals.

Today, as I continue to reorder my life, I often find my to-do list is much longer than my ability to fulfill it. Working, writing, organizing my house, managing our family spending plan, planning and preparing meals, spending time with my family and friends, working on our family plans, taking personal time, making gifts, reading... the list seems endless. Like most active people, I have a lot going on.

So now I find myself asking the familiar question: "I know I can't do it all right now, but what can I do?"

Intentionally planning what we can do helps establish healthy limits. For example, I would love to have a small vegetable garden. Gardening relaxes me. Growing some of our own food would be a good learning experience for our children, and it would save on our grocery bill. But this year I have too many other things going. Trying to establish beds, start seeds, plant the seedlings, and care for the home garden would turn my vision of pleasure into a quagmire of failure and stress. So that intention is on hold for now.

However, I could buy some established plants at the nursery and fill planter boxes and pots with herbs, bell peppers, and tomatoes. I could putter around my container gardens and realize some of the pleasure of gardening. So that became my goal.

This same sorting process helps us take the necessary steps to escape the rat race. Reordering our lives is not a quick-fix exercise. This is not a *Thirty-Day Plan to Move from Bedlam to Serenity!* Change is a process. Shifting our attitudes and reorienting our actions takes time. Our lives are much like huge ocean liners moving across the sea. There are no sharp or hairpin turns for the massive ships. Instead, the skipper guides the vessel around slowly and surely and soon begins traveling in the direction he wants it to go.

Perhaps you can't become debt-free immediately, but can you begin paying off your credit cards now? Maybe you can't organize a family dinner every night, but can you plan one family-night-at-home each week? Maybe you can't dedicate an entire week to evaluating and planning your life, but can you invest thirty minutes a day or one hour a week? Maybe you can't work out every day, but can you take a thirty-minute walk three days a week? Maybe you can't take a two-week vacation in Hawaii, but can you get away to a cabin on the lake for a three-day weekend? Maybe you can't feed all the hungry children in our world, but can you feed just one in your city?

Rather than "throwing the baby out with the bath water," consider breaking a project or goal into smaller steps or pieces and begin to move toward the solutions and benefits you seek.

DECIDE WHAT YOU *WON'T* DO

As you make decisions and set goals about what you'll do, you'll find yourself gaining control over your life and enjoying a tremendous reduction in stress. You'll gain even more composure if you *decide* what you won't do! For example, I have multiple interests. I find great pleasure when I write, draw, sew, knit, cross-stitch, and make things. I have a passion for books, study, and contemplation. I love people and like spending time with friends. I like homemaking, cooking, decorating, entertaining, and gardening. I enjoy my work, travel, and the arts.

Actually, I could probably fill about ten pages with lists of activities I like doing. But again, I can't do them all—and I certainly can't do several things at the same time with the kinds of results I like to achieve (I find great pleasure from doing *any* task well).

Again, I begin the sorting and selection process. As I'm deciding what I will do, I'm mentally creating limits at the same time and deciding what I will *not* do. For example, I decided to center my creative work on writing and paper. That means I'm making handmade greeting cards, postcards, stationery, posters, framed verses and prose, and other works of art that involve paper and words. In order to focus my efforts on this medium, I'm choosing to *not* do other crafts I enjoy. Next year I'll probably center my attention on quilting, knitting, or other handwork. The trick is to invoke my self-discipline to stay with my plan. Most of the time I'm successful.

What activities do you want to do? Do you want to volunteer at a shelter one day a month? Is there a language you want to learn? Are there clubs you want to join or a special interest group or book club you want to join?

We can realize our dreams when we intentionally plan for them.

WRITING GOALS ACCORDING TO YOUR
LIFE PURPOSE

Developing goals helps you transform your hopes and dreams into reality. For the greatest success in achieving goals, write them using good, sound, business principles. I learned a clever system for writing goals from George Sweeting, the former president of Moody Bible Institute and the author of several books. A busy man with many demands for his time and attention, Dr. Sweeting needed to institute some good habits if he was to complete all the things he wanted to do. He adopted the practice of writing S.M.A.R.T. goals. That is, goals that are

---

A Checklist for Evaluating Our Maturity

I will be mature when...

I do not automatically resent criticism because I realize that it may contain a suggestion for my improvement.

I know that self-pity is futile and childish—a way of placing blame for my disappointments on others.

I do not lose my temper readily or allow myself to "fly off the handle" about trivial matters.

I keep my head in emergencies and deal with them in a logical, reasonable fashion.

I accept responsibility for my actions and decisions and do not blame someone else when things go wrong.

I accept reasonable delays without impatience, realizing that I must adjust myself to the convenience of others.

I am a good loser, accepting defeat and disappointment without complaint or ill temper.

I do not worry unduly about things I can't do anything about.

I don't boast or show off, but when praised or complimented, I accept the words with grace and appreciation and without false modesty.

Specific, Measurable, Achievable, Reasonable, and Tangible.[4] This criteria embodies the most sound business principles for goal writing.

To increase our chances of actually realizing our goals, they must be specific. "I want to read more," is a goal, but it lacks punch and meaning. Consider the what, when, where, and how to develop the specific information needed to write an articulate goal. A specific way to write this goal would be: "I will read one fiction book and one non-fiction book from the current *New York Times* best-seller list each quarter of the coming year."

If you have specific books in mind, they could be men-

I applaud the achievement of others with sincere good will.

I rejoice in the good fortune and success of others because I have outgrown petty jealousy and envy.

I listen courteously to the opinions of others and even when they hold opposing views, I do not enter into hostile arguments.

I don't find fault in "every little thing" or criticize people who do things I may not approve of.

I make reasonable plans for my activities and try to carry them out in orderly fashion; I don't do things on the spur of the moment without due consideration.

I show spiritual understanding by:

- accepting the fact that God has an important place in my life;
- realizing I am part of humankind as a whole, that people have much to give me, and that I have an obligation to share with others the gifts that have been bestowed on me;
- obeying the Golden Rule to "do unto others as I would have them do unto me."

tioned in the goal: "I will read *Plain and Simple* by Sue Bender on my vacation in September."

The only way you can know if you have or have not achieved your goals is to write them with *measurable* results. Again, the measurements should be specific. "I will lose weight," is not measurable. Do you mean you will lose one pound or ten pounds? Will you keep the weight loss for a week or will you try to maintain it? Write your goals so you can measure how close you get to the standards you set.

Another way to write that goal would be, "On August 1, I will adopt the Dr. Dean Ornish low-fat weight-loss diet until I weigh one hundred twenty pounds, at which time I will switch to his low-fat maintenance diet to maintain that weight for at least six months."

When we write our goals, we need to make sure they are achievable. We also must make sure we have the control to assure our completion of the goal. "I will become the vice president of marketing for ABC Electronics by January," is specific and measurable. But gaining this position depends on the actions of other people. Achieving it is not entirely up to the goal setter.

It would be better to write, "This summer I will take two night classes in marketing; I will update my resumé; and I will apply for the position of vice president of marketing for ABC Electronics by January." All of these steps are in your control. They are all achievable.

Meeting the requirement of *reasonable* goals is similar to *achievable* goals, but it also guides us to keep our goals within realistic limits. "I will lose twelve pounds before leaving on my Hawaiian vacation next month," is not a reasonable goal (within healthy standards). Even if you could go on a crash diet and lose the weight, doing so would be counter to your commitment to healthy living. Make sure your goals are reasonable.

Tangible gives clarity and definition to your goals. A goal such as, "I will be *happier* next year," is not tangible. Instead, define those activities that make you happy and then write goals that include them. Ask yourself, "What makes me happy?" Perhaps it's spending time with friends. Your goal would read, "Each month, for the next twelve months, I will go on one outing with at least one of my friends." Now you can plan for a tangible or defined event.

Try to memorize the acronym of S.M.A.R.T. and then apply it when you write your goals.

REFLECTIVE GOALS

Before you begin writing your goals, review your purpose in life by reading your personal mission statement. Then ask yourself what you can do to fulfill your life mission. Write goals that reflect your purpose, principles, and values. Consider the following areas:

Self-care. What can you do to care for yourself that would bring you joy and pleasure? Could you plan a two-day get-away at a retreat center? Could you make a weekly date with yourself to visit an art gallery or the library? What are those simple pleasures that are special just for you? Write a goal and plan to care for yourself.

Self-improvement. Could you improve your organizational skills? Do you have some unresolved issues that could be solved with the help of a counselor? Would you like to learn a foreign language? Plan for your self-improvement.

Spiritual growth. Do you still wonder if God is for real? Would you like to start going to church? Would you like to take up daily devotions or meditation? Develop a S.M.A.R.T. goal.

Intellectual growth. How can you exercise and stretch your mind? Can you sign up for a lecture series at your local community college or a university extension program? Can you choose a topic and check out books at the library? Can you join a monthly study group or a computer user group?

Physical improvement. How's your diet, your exercise, your health? Consider new habits you can develop (or some you can drop) that will improve your health and make you feel better. Write a goal.

Relationships. Consider family members, friends, work associates. Are there some activities you can plan to help strengthen your important relationships?

Home improvement. Does the carpet need cleaning? The couch need new slip covers? What are ways you can make your home better for you, your family, and your friends? Write a S.M.A.R.T. goal.

Celebrations. How do you want to celebrate your birthday? Is there an important anniversary coming up? How about Christmas? Think about the ways you celebrate life and make plans for fulfilling and meaningful experiences.

Work. Do you like your job? Do you work too many or too few hours? Are there new skills or habits you can develop to improve your output?

Entertainment. Do you like the theater? Are there movies you want to see? Do you want to entertain friends in your home?

Recreation. All work and no play? Plan some times of fun and relaxation to give yourself a rest.

Education. Is there a class you've always wanted to take? A degree you want to earn? A skill you want to master? Check into classes and plan for enrollment.

Literature. How many times have you said, "Oh, I wish I had more time to read"? Well, plan for it! What books do you want to read this year? Do you want to read to your children? Have you considered starting or joining a reading group or organizing a weekend reading retreat?

Creating art. Your mind is full of creative ideas! What kinds of crafts or art projects do you enjoy? Is there a new art form you would like to try? Would you like to master a skill you've been developing for many years?

Service. Do you have skills that can improve the lives of others? How about organizing a coat and blanket drive? Serving dinner at a soup kitchen? Making a grocery shopping trip especially for homeless children?

Charity. Would you like to make giving a regular part of your financial plan? Choose two or three organizations that support causes that interest you. Plan monthly, quarterly, or annual gifts into your budget.

Finances. Would you like to pay off all debt? Do you need to earn some extra income for a special project? Would you like your spending to reflect your principles and values? Make a plan. Develop S.M.A.R.T. goals.

Time. So much to do—so little time? Can you cut out activities that are inconsistent with your priorities? Can you improve your scheduling? Can you adopt time-saving tips that will provide more relaxation and less stress?

Habits. Are there habits you want to break? Are there healthy habits you want to develop? Think about habits you have and consider their value.

Disciplines. Would you like to pray regularly? Begin an exercise routine? Control your spending, eating, gossiping? What self-disciplines do you want to adopt?

Limits. Are there areas of your life that seem out of control? Do you limit the amount of time you watch television? Do you limit your work time? How about the food you eat, the dollars you spend, or the speed you drive? Adopt healthy limits.

These are just some of the areas to consider for goal setting. Think about the way you spend your time, the special needs and activities in which you're involved. Think about your goals.

ANNUAL GOALS

Most of us make a few resolutions at the beginning of a new year. That's a natural time to look back at our past and consider our future. But we don't need to wait for the new year to begin writing our goals. We can take a snapshot of our life right now and make some decisions about what we want to accomplish.

Most successful companies have annual planning meetings. World Concern has employees in more than thirty-five countries around the world. Every October, the area directors for Africa, Asia, and Latin America meet for two weeks with other World Concern administrators and managers to review their programs, investigate and study trends, and develop plans for the coming fiscal year (which runs from July 1 to June 30). They come together again in May to finalize goals and establish their annual budgets.

Our lives and the way we lead them are very much like a business, especially if we want to live intentionally to achieve our life purpose. That's why Fred and I have our annual meeting.

Fred and I gained so much insight during our Lake Chelan excursion that we make sure we have one week away each year. We reserve this time for planning our future, assessing our progress, and setting new sights. No kids and no friends allowed. This is our family business meeting—and the heads-of-state are the only invited guests. It's a time for just the two of us to go away, quiet our spirits, and discover where we will go for our future.

I realize not everyone can take week-long retreats, but most people can plan for a few days or an overnight. If that's not possible for you now, set aside a few evenings or mornings to talk about what you want to do in the coming year.

LOOKING INTO THE FUTURE

I'm one of those bring-out-the-charts-and-graphs visual types. I think more clearly with pictures or sketches than I do with obscure theories. When Fred and I started our planning process, I developed a chart that helped me "look" into our future so we could set some long-term goals.

I took a sheet of the now-familiar notebook paper and drew three rows of four boxes. I labeled each box with consecutive years, beginning with the current year. In each box, I added the initials of each member of the family to whom Fred and I still had primary responsibility (when our kids fly the coop, we encourage them to build strong muscles so they can keep flying—no homing pigeons, please). After the initial of each person, I added the age or the year in school each person would be at the beginning of that year.

Here's an example of four years. I used ages for Fred and myself. I used school grades for Crista, Seth and Dawit. Our other daughter, Kirsten, is living securely on her own, so she's off the chart.

After I had completed twelve boxes with this information, I added benchmarks to each box. For example, I noted when each of the kids could graduate from high school and college. I indicated the year when Fred and I wanted to be free of debt. I used the chart to plan when it would be feasible to accept an overseas assignment, taking into account when Dawit would be through with high school and most likely living in a college dormitory. I remember when I was a kid and felt as if the year 2000 was light-years away—surprise, time passes whether we're having fun or not! This chart smacks with reality and helps us look into the future for our planning process!

19___	19___	19___	19___
F-49	F-50	F-51	F-52
S-43	S-44	S-45	S-46
C-Ju.	C-Sr.		
S-12	S-Fr.	S-So.	S-Ju.
D-4	D-5	D-6	D-7

I also use the chart to foresee major purchases such as replacing an automobile, roofing or painting the house, and college tuition. Fred's car will need replacing in five or six more years. I can put that on our chart so we can begin saving now to pay cash when the time comes. The chart serves as an excellent tool as we develop spending plans, prepare for financial independence, establish goals, and work to turn our hopes and dreams into reality.

YOUR TURN

1. Review the work you've done to this point. Read your notes and make a list of the things you would like to accomplish

in your lifetime.

2. Using the S.M.A.R.T. method, write goals for each dream, plan, and hope.

3. Think about the things you will need to accomplish this year to reach your future goals. Write specific goals for the coming twelve months.

4. Consider the areas of your life where you would like to focus your change. Write goals for those areas.

5. File all your information in your notebook under "How I Want To Live."

> "Give me a young man in whom there is something of the old, and an old man in whom there is something of the young. Guided so, a man may grow old in body but never in mind."[5]
>
> **Marcus Tullius Cicero**

9

Your Personal Escape Route

If you do not sow in the spring
you will not reap in the autumn.

Irish Proverb

You've done a lot of work to this point, and I hope you've made some exciting and perhaps even surprising discoveries about yourself and your life. The knowledge about the real you and the plans you've made for your future have given you a new sense of security, confidence, and encouragement. You're just about ready to forge into the beautiful forest that awaits you. You've done the exercises to prepare your body, mind, and spirit... and now you need to pack just a few more things into your backpack.

These aren't survival tools; you already have those resting inside your heart. These are merely implements that can help you travel the direction you want to go. These instruments are universal, but you will tailor them to meet your specific and unique needs:

1. Spending Plan
2. Calendars
3. Journal
4. Notebooks

DEBT, DEBT, AND MORE DEBT

You don't need to be an economist to know that we Americans are up to our eyeballs in debt. Credit has allowed people to live substantially beyond their means... and even our government has developed a severe case of spending beyond our country's means, resulting in a $3 trillion budget deficit—a number higher than I can fathom.

In a 1993 report published by the Bureau of Economic Analysis, the amount of debt Americans carry, compared with their income, has soared over the last forty years. In fact, the average amount of debt climbed 20 percent between 1980 and 1992. Americans love to spend money, even if we don't have it. Going to the mall has replaced baseball as our national sport!

In the meantime, our cupboards, drawers, closets, basements, attics, and garages are packed with "stuff." We have yard sales to get rid of what we don't need... so we can make money to buy more of what we don't need! Just look around your house at all the stuff you've accumulated that you rarely, if ever, use. If you're like me, you have to raise your hand and say, "Guilty as charged."

Credit card debt continues to climb. Financial consultants report that significantly high credit card debt used to range from $30,000 to $40,000. Now they counsel many people with $60,000 to $100,000 accumulated on ten, twenty, or even thirty credit cards. These people are from all levels of employment—managers and vice presidents of companies on down through the rank and file.

Credit and financial counselors advise consumers to watch out for these warning signs. If you do any of the following, you may be getting over your head in debt:

- Making only minimum payments on your credit card debts
- Getting cash advances on your credit cards to pay off other debts
- Buying groceries on credit
- Having no money left after you've paid the month's bills

- Going shopping if you are bored or depressed—particularly on credit
- Regularly requesting higher credit card limits
- Seeking a debt consolidation loan
- Drawing repeatedly on a home-equity line of credit
- Having your wages garnished

One freeing step to get out of the rat race is to pay off your debt—including credit cards, automobiles, and even mortgages! Here are a few options you can consider:

1. List all your debts, grouping according to type (credit cards, medical bills, mortgages, auto loans, etc.).
2. List your credit cards and your other debts in each category in the order of highest interest charged (you can get this information from your net worth worksheet).
3. Cut down on your spending; put your credit cards in a drawer, or cut them up, so you don't use them (you may want to save one card for mail order purchases—but limit purchases to only necessary items); pay down the card with the highest interest rate while making minimum payments on the other cards.
4. Make a vow to pay cash for everything!
5. After your cards are paid off, tackle the next consumer debt. Perhaps your car, an old student loan, or a furniture purchase you put on a contract.
6. Finally, begin making extra principal payments on your mortgage, putting all extra money directly toward the principal.

Now, you may be saying, "What about my income tax deductions?" But if you pencil out the figures, you'll see the money you save on interest far exceeds the extra amount you will pay Uncle Sam—and don't forget the money and peace of mind you'll have when you are debt-free.

Joe Dominguez, one of the authors of the best-selling book,

Your Money or Your Life, has presented his seminar called "Transforming Your Relationship with Money and Achieving Financial Independence" to more than 30,000 men and women. He reports that many middle-class families who undertake the goal to become debt-free and financially independent (meaning they no longer have to work for money) find it takes from seven to ten years to do so. Those who can increase their income (without jeopardizing health, ethics, or relationships) while decreasing expenses, can achieve their goal faster.

Can you imagine not having debt? Think about how it would change your life... then write your plan. You can do it—and by the way, you can still call yourself an American!

DETERMINE YOUR INCOME-DEBT RATIO

Have you ever wondered when you have too much debt? This may help answer your question. I saw this tip by my favorite financial advisor, Jane Bryant Quinn. I've developed a chart, using her directions[1], to help figure debt limit.

To determine how much debt you can safely carry, list all your monthly payments (excluding mortgage) on debts that will take more than six months to pay off. You can use the information you gathered when you developed your net worth statement.

Divide your debt total by your monthly gross income to find out the percentage of your debt. You can then use that percentage rate to see where you are on the safety scale.

Monthly Debt	Amount
_____	_____
_____	_____
_____	_____
_____	_____
_____	_____
_____	_____
_____	_____

Total: _____

(divide by your regular monthly gross income) _____

Debt-to-income ratio: _____

1 - 15%: you're within OK limits

15 - 20%: be careful!

20 - 35%: you're flirting with disaster

35 - 50%: you're in serious trouble

50% +: you're headed for bankruptcy

Sensible Advice That Still Works

1. Pay yourself first. If you began investing just $100 every month at age thirty, when you reached sixty-five you would have more than $107,000 (assumes 9 percent annual return). Start saving today.

2. Use unit pricing when you shop for groceries. Children's cookies in a small decorated box were $6.32/pound; a larger bag with cookies shaped like Bugs Bunny were $3.66/pound; those shaped like zoo animals were $2.38/pound; and another brand of zoo animals were $2.12/pound. Fresh chicken breasts were $2.29/pound; plain crackers were $6.79/pound. Unit pricing adds perspective to your shopping!

3. Deal with small things before they turn into big ones. This is true for personal issues, family relationships, financial management, gardening, cleaning, and more.

4. Plan ahead. Planning provides more choices and increased control. Whether it's a dinner party, a vacation, an important work project or a holiday celebration, planning enables you to be more creative and fine-tune your efforts.

SPENDING PLAN

You'll find that a plan for how you will spend your hard-earned dollars will be one of the most valuable tools you'll use on your journey out of the rat race. Now that you have determined where you are (from the baseline study of your spending habits and your net worth), you can make a plan for where you want to go.

I suggest going to your local bookstore to browse through books about personal financial management. I suggest these two books as absolute musts for anyone wanting to gain control of their money so they can finance their dreams:

Making the Most of Your Money, by Jane Bryant Quinn (Simon and Schuster, $27.50)

Your Money or Your Life, by Joe Dominguez and Vicki Robin (Viking, $20.00 hardback, $11.00 paperback)

Both offer detailed financial management planning models, but they vary in their approach. I suggest gleaning the best from both books and setting up systems that are best for you.

One thing is sure: keeping detailed financial records and developing a specific plan for your spending is a key to your success. You are in the business of life. You are the chief executive officer, and if you want success, you must use the principles and tools to take you there. Develop a plan to align your spending with your long-term goals, your principles, and your values. Decide how your dollars will leave your hands rather than letting the greenbacks slip through your fingers or go up in smoke.

TALKING ON PAPER

Changing your life will require discipline. After all, rats are creatures of habit and when we want out of the race, we need to form new habits. One of the disciplines that will help keep you on the path you've chosen is journaling.

A journal is a book just for you. It's a private place where you can "think things through" as you fill the pages with your words. You may want to add your thoughts to your notebook, but I prefer to keep my journals separate. Committing our intangible thoughts to paper helps bring clarity and understanding to our minds. I find journaling to be a wonderful meeting place with God. As I write about my thoughts, concerns, frustrations, or dreams, I feel as if I'm tapping into God's wisdom. My journal is like "conversation on paper" as I pour out my feelings and seek his direction for my life. It is almost mystical as I increase in understanding and work toward solutions.

In the spring of 1993, I purchased an inexpensive set of colored pencils and started sketching in my journal to visualize some of the word pictures I penned on the pages. I'm no great artist, and that's OK because the images are only for me. Even with my simple drawings, the process of sketching my thoughts brings an even deeper understanding to the issues I'm writing about. My journaling expands from writing thoughts to a type of meditation.

CALENDARS

With our busy schedules, good working calendars are a must. As you'll notice, I used the word "working." That's because as you begin filling in your calendar's pages with all the details you've been trying to store in your head, your tool will almost come alive. You'll soon learn you can't live without it! It's dynamic—it changes constantly.

There are four rules for keeping a good calendar:

Rule #1: USE ONLY ONE PERSONAL CALENDAR. This is the most important rule about calendars, yet most people try to use two or three. More than one calendar causes you to worry about transferring information, keeping all calendars updated, and double-booking yourself. Use the same calendar at the office for business appointments and at home for family and personal business.

Rule #2: CHOOSE A CALENDAR THAT FITS YOU. Go to an office supply store and look at the different types of calendars offered. Think about the type of information you need to remember. Make sure the calendar you choose has space to record appointments and notes as well as space for errands, projects, and phone calls. The calendar should be small enough to carry with you at all times.

Rule #3: WRITE DOWN EVERYTHING. Free your mind by writing down information in your calendar. Even if you have a lunch meeting every Wednesday, write it down. If you have season tickets to concerts, plays, or sporting events, transfer the schedules to your calendar as soon as they are announced. It's too easy to forget the date when you're scheduling other appointments.

Rule #4: REVIEW YOUR CALENDAR. Look at your calendar every day to see what you need to do that day. Also, look at the next week to see what lies ahead. Review your calendar with your family to coordinate with their schedules. My husband and I frequently compare and coordinate our calendars. We also review our calendars at our family meetings so the children are aware of travel plans, outings, etc., and so we can add their dates to ours (baseball games, school and church events, outings).

My calendar (a DayRunner) has 5 1/2" x 8 1/2" pages in a three-ring binder. It includes a month-at-a-glance, daily to-do sheets, expense records, notes, and a name and address directory.

Our family is very active. I've found using a wall calendar with a full year on it useful to assure better communication among all of us (this is the only exception to the one calendar rule). On the calendar are travel plans, sporting events, and other happenings that involve the whole family. We keep it current by updating it at our weekly family meetings.

I also keep a master birthday list in my computer (you can also use a birthday book). Once each year I add the birthdays to my calendar so I can remember to send cards, call with birthday greetings, or plan special little celebrations.

Sometimes I schedule private time: a couple hours each week, a day, a month, or a weekend every quarter. I've found that being attentive to my family has its drawback: I'm constantly in demand! So taking care of myself by providing time out is essential to my health. I try to plan for refreshment time to be alone with no demands. Plan for your own quiet time according to whatever your schedule can bear.

Choose whatever plan works best for you. You'll find a good calendar system enables you to plan ahead much better. You'll be in better control of your time, and rarely will you forget or miss appointments.

I've also found other tools that help me keep information organized and accessible. That's why I've earned the distinguished title of...

THE THREE-RING NOTEBOOK QUEEN

There's no getting around it. Our family is busy. With two active boys in a home headed by two professional parents, we have a lot going on. So keeping track of information, organizing lists, data, and references, and then making sure everyone knows where they can find things is really important. I've found the best way to do that is through inexpensive, colored, three-ring binders. I have different notebooks for:

NAMES AND NUMBERS. One of the most frequently accessed notebooks is the one near our kitchen telephone. It's a brown, half-inch-ring binder that holds 8 1/2" x 11" sheets of paper. That's where we keep the list of our friends, their addresses, and telephone numbers. We also list Fred's coworkers along with their addresses and telephone numbers. We have telephone numbers of our favorite restaurants, family members, doctors, and emergency numbers. On another page we have lists of favorite bookstores, the neighborhood hardware store, the dog groomer, the barber and hair-dresser, and other places of business whose numbers we need. We also keep the boys' sporting event schedules in the book along with coaches' and players' names and numbers.

This book saves us from having to repeatedly look up the numbers in the telephone directories, and its central location makes the information easy and quick to access.

MEAL PLANNING. To save time and money, I plan our dinner menus on a fourteen-day rotating schedule. You guessed it, I keep the menus in a three-ring notebook (maroon) along

Eating Out

E ating away from home isn't always cheap. When you add it all up, you may find the amount of money you spend on snacks, lunches, and beverages is much higher than you expected. If you spend $1.75 on a latti each morning before work, your annual total adds up to $420. Now add lunches with workmates (at a minimum cost of $4.50, but my guess is that most people are closer to $7.50 or more) for another $1,080, and suddenly you've spent $1,500. Kick in snacks from the vending machine at $.75 a crack, which adds an additional $180, for a total of $1,680 (what do you mean you can't afford a vacation?).

While you have to eat during the day... and coffee drinks and snacks are nice for breaks... can you cut back and save toward one of your dreams?

with copies of each recipe and comments about their outcome (next I'll graduate to the type of notebook salespeople use for presentations because it can sit up on my counter while I'm using the recipe).

I copy all the recipes on 8 1/2" x 11" sheets of paper to maintain order. I keep some in sheet protectors if I need to see both sides, like those clipped from magazines or newspapers. Then I sort the menus and their recipes in the order of the days they'll be prepared. When I plan my trip to the grocery store, I merely flip through the recipes and make my list. When I want to change the meal rotation, it's just a matter of moving recipes around or adding new ones that we want to try (more about this in the next chapter).

NEWSLETTERS. I like and use newsletters. I used to keep them in stacks, then in cardboard magazine holders, and now in easy to store three-ring binders. I use the kind of notebooks that have a clear vinyl pocket on the front which allows me to slip a cover page inside. These notebooks work especially well because I can keep the newsletters in chronological order. I also use little removable tabs made by 3-M for easy access (you can get them in a variety of colors at office supply stores). I leave the newsletters out to share with family members and guests, knowing they will stay in order and in good condition because of the notebook.

REFERENCE BOOK. I am also a lover of magazines. Several years ago, I started topic notebooks that hold articles I want to save. Again, the notebooks protect the pages and keep them orderly. For most applications, they work much better than files. These notebooks are all the same color (black) with a label on the spine to title the contents (crafts, time and money, fitness and health, etc.). I try to set aside a time each month to go through my stack of magazines and pull out articles, recipes and other pages that I want to save. I then toss the rest of the magazine in the recycle bin. It's a great way to cut down on clutter.

CHRISTMAS NOTEBOOK. Sad, but true, Christmas has become one of the top stress producers in people's lives. It's especially difficult on women as Jo Robinson and Jean Coppock Staeheli point out in their best-selling survival guide, *Unplug the Christmas Machine*[2].

My favorite part of Christmas is getting ready for the celebration, but I don't like going crazy over it. My Christmas notebook is one of the most valuable gifts I've made for myself, and it saves me many hours of time and loads upon loads of stress.

I use a standard three-ring binder with one-inch rings. Mine is an appropriate Christmas green with pockets in the inside covers. I have five dividers:

Calendar   Menu   To-do

Addresses   Santa

Before I ever leave the house to start shopping, I list the people to whom we want to give gifts. I've found it especially helpful to make a planning chart like this one:

Name	Gift Ideas	Approx. $ amount	Notes	Store	Day/Rt.
Adam	Fire engine	$25.00	Tyco	Costco	
John	Bird House	$18.00	hand-crafted	Pike Place Market	
Carol	Robe	$45.00	size 10, long, green or blue	Nordstrom	

Fred and I think of gift ideas for each person, budget an amount, and note where the item can be purchased. If we're planning on making the gift, we list the items and stores for supplies. I also add notes like sizes, brands, or colors so we don't have to guess when we get to the stores. The final step is to plan the shopping route and number the locations in the order we'll travel. I put my chart in the Santa section of my notebook. If we've seen an item in a store ad, we clip it and keep it in one of the cover pockets so we can refer to it when we shop.

We also use the chart to order whatever we can from mail-order catalogs. One year, we purchased all but five gifts from catalogs—that's quite a feat because we exchange many gifts with our large, extended family and many friends.

In the address section of the notebook, I keep the addresses and phone numbers of those to whom we will send gifts (some shipping services require the telephone number of the recipient). Most stores can mail gifts—and some even offer free shipping!

I keep a business-sized envelope in the back pocket of the notebook to keep track of receipts. After purchasing an item, I write the gift recipient's name on the back of the receipt and slip it into the envelope (this keeps it handy in the event of exchange or return). I also write the amount of the purchase on the front of the envelope and keep a running total of our purchases (it's amazing how fast we can overspend if we're not keeping track). I also refer to the gift list when I purchase wrapping paper, gift cards, and ribbons—which I accomplish in one stop.

In the address section, I keep a list of the names and addresses of those who will receive our annual Christmas letter (I keep all this on my computer, which makes it very handy). I then update the list with address changes taken from envelopes we receive with cards and letters from friends and associates. After the first of the year, I update my computer list so it's ready when we send our letters the following year.

I have a master to-do list that I use to make sure everything gets done. I also give this list to Fred and the boys so they can decide the ways they'll help out (delegating is a key part of unplugging the Christmas machine).

I enter all holiday events on a master calendar. I also enter dates involving the whole family: decorating the house, decorating the tree, producing our Christmas letter, and baking. This visual tool captures all the planned activities and helps me get real about what I can accomplish. As soon as I sense the slightest inkling of stress—I start to consider what I can eliminate. I figure, if I feel the stress just thinking about it while it's just on paper, I'll certainly experience mega-stress when I'm trying to follow through.

Finally, my menu section holds the Christmas dinner menu, copies of all the recipes I'll use, my shopping and pantry list, and my plan of attack—including actual times (see fourteen-day-menu-planning in next chapter).

This all may sound like a lot of work and fanatical detail.

From the Heart

Birthdays, anniversaries, Valentine's Day, and Christmas are some of our favorite celebrations. But with four children, one grandchild, and a fairly large extended family, the number of gifts we give is sizable. Add our friends and their children and the number (and the budget line) can really add up! Here are some ideas that help reduce the cost but at the same time increase the value of the gift:

1. Books On Tape: Purchase a book that would be especially appreciated by a child and then read it aloud into a cassette player. Personalize the reading by saying things like, "Joel, turn the page now." or "Lauren, does that look like your bear?" Wrap the book, the tape and a photo of you together in a sturdy box that can be used for future storage.

2. Heirlooms: Do you enjoy making things like wooden toys, cross-stitch, or quilts? Maybe you paint or draw? Think about special ways you can use your talents to create little treasures that will be kept for years to come.

But I can't come close to describing the sense of peace and joy I'm able to experience because I've eliminated the majority of stress associated with the holiday. Because I have a plan, I'm able to do those activities that are important to me. I can center on the true meaning of Christmas. And my husband and kids all love it because I don't yell, kick, bite, scream, or whine at them!

The extra planning time invested in my Christmas notebook multiplies itself into hours and hours of enjoyment. After Christmas, the book gets filed away, and I pull it out again the next year. Everything is handy, in one place, and complete. Pretty cool, I have to admit!

Developing helpful tools to organize mundane and frequently-

I'm in the process of making old-fashioned beaded pincushions which I hope will be enjoyed.

3. Plant a Tree: Giving a tree, a rose bush, or another plant serves as a growing reminder of your special gift of love. Include a poem to the gift tag as an added bonus.

4. Time-In-A-Bottle: Plan a special outing like a visit to the museum or a trip to the zoo. Write the details on a piece of paper, then roll it up and put it into a special bottle decorated with ribbons and bows (you can purchase nice bottles in kitchen supply stores or import shops).

5. Words: Write a poem or a special letter to your loved one. Frame it, using a double matte so you can include their photograph or a picture of the two of you together.

6. Refrigerator Art: Everyone uses magnets on their fridge. Be creative! Place a special photo in a plastic photo frame with a magnet on the back. Purchase magnets at a craft store and then personalize them by gluing shells, buttons, silk roses, friendly plastic creations, or other decorations on them.

repeated tasks frees us to use our time, energy, and creativity in areas that are more important to us. The investment of time and resources to develop the tools yields high returns as I continue to use my tools time and time again.

YOUR TURN

1. Look at your calendar. Does it provide the information you need in an efficient, easy-to-access manner? Talk to friends or associates about the calendars they use. See what they like and what they have found unnecessary. Then think about the types of information you need to have with you all the time. Invest in a serviceable calendar that will meet your unique needs.

2. What other types of information do you need to access frequently? Take some time and list the reference tools that will make your life easier. Perhaps notecards would meet your needs better than a three-ring binder. Computers are great for developing and updating these tools.

3. Would reference notebooks or a Christmas notebook help organize the information you want to save and retrieve? What other tools would be helpful? Consider your needs and then visit the local discount office supply store and begin developing your system. By the way, I don't mind sharing my notebook queen crown with you!

10

Packing the Essentials

Opportunities are usually disguised as hard work,
so most people don't recognize them.

Ann Landers

Since I started writing the newsletter, I've become a magnet for cost- and time-saving ideas as well as for tips on better living. If I tried to pass along everything I've collected, this little paperback would turn into volumes! But there are five areas we all have in common. I want to give you some tools you can begin using right away as you find ways to de-stress and reorder your life. I encourage you to invest the time to set up these systems for you and your family. The hours you'll save and the peace of mind and control you'll gain will bring significant payoffs in the future.

Try the tips I offer here for these major task areas of your life. Like the Nike ads preach: JUST DO IT!

We all have to:

1. Eat

2. Sleep

3. Get dressed (my friend Susie might argue with this point)

4. Get along with those we live with

5. Pay our bills

6. File the volumes of papers we have to save

FOURTEEN-DAY MEAL PLAN

Of all the ways I've tried to organize my daily life, the four-teen-day meal plan has saved the greatest amount in time and money. The investment of time to develop my book is well worth it! It took me a while to get fourteen complete menus together, so you may want to start by planning just one week, then adding as you go. Using this plan has made daily meal preparation a pleasant experience. I frequently recruit family members to help me prepare the meal, not so much because I need the help, but because it's a fun time to relate. I'd love to hear your mealtime tips, so please write. Until then, *bon appétit*!

Supplies:

- Three-ring notebook (I use a binder with 1" rings)
- Dividers (I use the first fourteen pages of a set of numbered dividers that come with pages numbered from 1-31. They're available at office supply stores. You can also use colored paper.)
- Paper (read steps first to see what works for you)

Steps:

1. *Select fourteen entrees* that you and your family will enjoy. I try to include a few fuller entrees for Sunday dinners and times when we may have company.

2. *Plan menus around each entree.* I keep in mind dietary needs, budgeting, and what foods are in season.

3. *Copy the recipes* on 8 1/2" x 11" paper. This is especially

helpful for recipes out of cookbooks. Because my office is in my home, I have a copier right here. I also type some on my computer. But recipes also can be copied at a copy center or library, or if you're really energetic you can hand-write them. You may want to cut recipes from magazines or newspapers and paste or tape them to a sheet of paper. I've also used clear plastic pages to hold recipes I've clipped (pages available at office supply stores).

4. *Paper clip together all recipes* for each menu.

5. *Develop a cover sheet for each menu* which includes the menu, shopping list, pantry list, and the game plan (the order of steps you or someone else can take to prepare the meal). If you don't use individual dividers, prepare your cover sheets on colored paper to serve as visual dividers.

6. *Schedule each menu* over the coming fourteen-day period while considering your calendar of planned events or meetings. Place the cover sheets along with the recipes in your three-ring binder in the appropriate order (you can eliminate the paper clips at this point). I also like to list the menus on a calendar which I keep on my refrigerator for easy reference (not a necessity, but I find it handy).

7. *Plan your weekly grocery list* by reviewing the cover sheets for the coming week. Check your pantry to make sure you have an adequate supply for all the pantry items listed.

8. *Prepare your meals* using your cover sheets and the recipes. Make notes of changes or additions.

9. *Move the pages to the back of the notebook* after completing the preparation and making all necessary notes.

10. After you've completed the fourteen days, *reschedule all the menus you liked, and add new menus if you choose.* Keep those menus not used in a file or in the back of your book for the future.

The great advantage of my Fourteen-Day Meal Plan Book is

that everything is handy and in one place. I don't have to wonder where I saw the recipe, nor do I have several cookbooks spread out on my counter. It's also a great way to share recipes with friends or to use the library as a resource for new culinary masterpieces. The menus have the primary dishes listed, but I often add olives, pickles, and other relishes. We're not big bread eaters (except at breakfast and lunch) so that's why you don't see rolls added to the menus.

Vegetable Chili and Corn Bread

Shopping List

2 green bell peppers	2 16 oz. cans pinto beans
1 yellow onion	2 16 oz. cans black beans
1 zucchini	2 16 oz. cans tomatoes
1 yellow squash	1 package frozen corn
1 4 oz. can mild green chilies	1 package corn bread mix

Pantry List:

salad oil	ground red peppers	chili powder
eggs	sugar	milk
salt		

Game Plan:

1. Prepare vegetables for chili
2. Sauté peppers and onions
3. Add peppers and squash
4. Follow remaining directions for chili recipe
5. While chili is cooking, prepare corn bread
6. Bake corn bread
7. When corn bread is done, serve.

Vegetable Chili

2 medium-sized green peppers, chopped
1 medium-sized yellow onion, chopped
1 medium-sized zucchini, sliced
1 medium-sized yellow squash, sliced
2 T salad oil (you can leave this out for low-fat diets and braise the veggies instead or use canola oil which is the best of oils for health-conscious folks)
2 T chili powder
1 T sugar
3/4 t salt
1/4 t ground red peppers
2 16 oz. cans tomatoes (juice and all)
2 16 oz. cans pinto beans (juice and all)
2 16 oz. cans black beans (juice and all)
1 4 oz. can mild green chilies
2 C corn kernels (frozen or fresh)

Chop and sauté in oil (or braise in water) peppers and onions. Add both squash, chili powder, sugar, salt, and ground red peppers. When soft but still firm, add tomatoes, beans, chilies (add juice and all), and corn. Bring to boil, reduce heat, and simmer for twenty minutes. Ready to eat now, but gets better with age. I added a small can of tomato paste and liked it. It kind of thickened up the liquid a little. Hope you enjoy it!

Yield: 4 generous servings

EYES WIDE-OPEN, BUT BRAIN SHUT-DOWN

Beep! Beep! Beep! "Oh, the alarm clock. It's too early to get up. I feel like I just went to sleep." Chances are, that's how you greeted the day this morning. Why? Because every day in America, millions of us who are caught in the rat race start our day tired. We haven't had enough sleep. But we have to get up anyway and start the day. Yawn.

While many of us don't act like it, our bodies require sleep. Sleep is just as necessary for health as food or drink. But do we give sleep the same priority? Not in today's rat race culture. We're just too busy. Mothers work all day, then go on to their second shift at home. We can go grocery shopping twenty-four hours a day. Many businesses run shifts around the clock. Most television stations offer programs from dusk to dawn.

One of the first things many of us cut from our busy schedules is sleep. We rise early to get to work on time, so we can fight traffic, rush off to meetings, hassle deadlines, pick a little, talk a little, pick-pick-pick, talk a lot, pick a little more. We go home to more activities and chores. Finally, we pour our weary bodies into bed, watch news-at-eleven and Jay's or Dave's monologue or Ted Koppel's *Nightline,* turn the tube off and we're out! No wonder that Beep! Beep! Beep! sounds in our ears so early!

For many, cutting back on sleep seems the only way to accomplish all there is to do. But more and more doctors and therapists are making the case that foregoing rest is a foolish and even dangerous concession. In fact, mounting evidence shows sleep deprivation has become one of our country's most pervasive health problems.

To function effectively, the average adult needs about eight hours of sleep a night. By that standard, millions of Americans are chronically sleep-deprived as we try to survive on six hours or less (research shows that only about 10 percent of the adult population needs more or less than eight hours of sleep each night).

Changes in our family lives contribute to the national sleep deficit. Working single parents and two-career families struggle to find time for their children or household chores. To fit it all in, they extend their waking hours. "By the time I get home, change my clothes, cook dinner, do a couple chores, and catch my breath, it's 9:00," complained a friend who is typical of a lot of working moms. "If we want to have any time with our kids, we find ourselves not getting them in bed until 10:00 or even later. Then, my husband and I want some time together and before we know it, it's nearly midnight! I have to be up by 6:00 to start getting us all ready to be out the door by 7:00."

Studies show that losing sleep night after night directly affects mental alertness and performance. In fact, officials from sleep-disorder clinics cite sleepiness as "one of the least recognized sources of disability in our society."[1] While people can walk, talk, see, and hear when they are sleep-deprived, they can't think clearly, make appropriate decisions, or maintain long attention spans.

Mental fatigue can be as foreboding as a heart attack. Evidence indicates that drowsiness is a leading cause of job related mishaps and traffic fatalities. Scientists report that "inadequate sleep is a major factor in human error, at least as important as drugs, alcohol and equipment failure."[2]

Day after day, week after week, month after month, we try to survive on less sleep. We might try to make it up on the weekends or during vacation times. But some researchers believe our sleep deficits build up over time, right along with the negative consequences. Sleep experts contend that most Americans no longer know what it feels like to be alert. They say sleepy people "go through the day in sort of a twilight zone. The eyes may be wide open, but the brain is partly shut down."[3]

When we are sleep-deprived, we not only lose our alertness, but we also lose our patience, our sense of humor, and our flexibility. Without adequate sleep, we become frustrated faster and are less able to keep our tempers in check, even over the slightest provocation, such as a driver cutting us off on the freeway or waiting in a long line at the bank or the grocery store. When we're chronically tired, we tend to nod off five minutes into a television program or within minutes of reading a book. My kids tease my husband about being like those dolls with the eyes that shut: as soon as his head lays back, his eyes close and he's out!

When we get enough rest, we can stay awake even during boring lectures, on long, straight roads, while reading dull reports, or after heavy meals. When we go to bed, it takes us ten or fifteen minutes before we go to sleep. We don't need an alarm clock to wake us in the morning. And when we do awake, we feel rested, alert, and ready to start a new day.

Check out your sleep situation by answering the following questions:

1. Do you need an alarm clock to wake up?

2. Do you fall asleep within five minutes of going to bed?

3. Do you wake up feeling tired and wanting more sleep?

4. Do you nod off or feel drowsy in the middle of the day?

5. Are you easily irritated or frustrated over "little things"?

If you answered yes to one or more of these questions, you may be suffering from sleep deprivation. Are there ways you can reorder your schedule or workload to give you more hours of sleep?

Use this 24-hour clock to chart out your typical day.

What time do you awake? When do you start work? Lunch time? Commute? Dinner? Social or family time? To bed? How many hours of sleep do you get on a typical day?

What changes would be necessary before you could get eight hours of sleep each night? Write them down. Do you want to change? If not, do you believe you may suffer the consequences? What changes can you make in the near future so you can be more rested? Can you work toward changing your

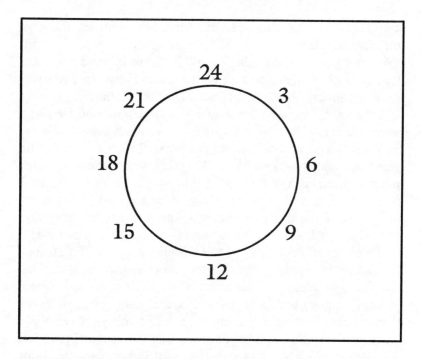

lifestyle so you can get the sleep your body and mind requires to be healthy, alert, and rested? Can you turn the television off or perhaps forego watching it during the week to allow for more time? If you find you have the time to sleep, but you're unable to sleep well, consider contacting one of the many sleep clinics or research centers in our country.

Start today. Take the steps out of the rat race that you need to take to make sure you're getting the sleep your body and mind are pleading for you to give them. And think of how great you'll feel when you're rested, alert, and in good spirits!

$3.25 PER WEAR

My friend, Ruth Douglas, is not only a classy lady, but she's also smart (a great combination). Several years ago when I was complaining about the high price of a pair of shoes, she gave me a great piece of advice. I've used it ever since. She said, "When I purchase clothing, I try to think beyond the price tag. Instead, I think about price-per-wear. How often will you wear the shoes? Now, do you think they're worth it?"

I thought, *Because these shoes are so basic and with the way I dress, I'll probably wear them about three times a week. They're well-made and will last about two years.* In other words, the pair I was about to spend $120 for (very well-made basic black pumps) actually cost me about thirty-eight cents each time I would wear them (figuring I would wear them about three times a week for about two years before they needed replacing. Actually, they lasted three years and then I had them resoled).

This calculation helps put the amount we are willing to pay for clothes into perspective. It's especially handy when we shop for the core pieces of our wardrobes. For example, I have a jacket that goes with a lot of things, including jeans, skirts, or dress slacks. I figure my cost to be about thirty-six cents per wear. On the other hand, I have another jacket that I paid less money for, but it's not as versatile. That jacket costs me about $3.25 per wear.

Thinking about price-per-wear makes us think twice about style, color, quality, and how an article works with what we already have.

This is also a handy trick when purchasing accessories and children's clothes. I've expanded the practice to other purchases such as small appliances, dinner ware, linens, kitchen gadgets, CDs, videos, garden equipment, etc. My kids are on the same track for the clothes they purchase and for their sports equipment.

Next time you're pondering the purchase price of a garment, think about the number of times you'll use the item. Divide that number into the price to come up with your price-per-wear. You may be dressing for less than you think!

TALK, TALK, TALK, TALK A LOT, TALK A LITTLE MORE

While marriage and family counselors may take different approaches to solving relationship problems, there is one foundation on which all agree: Good communication is the key to good relationships and especially critical for couples and families.

Unfortunately, many of us didn't learn good communication skills when we were growing up. Perhaps we came from families with a "no talk rule" where members ignored troublesome issues in hopes they would just fade away or disappear. Maybe our families communicated, but not in the healthiest of ways—as happens when one or both parents are controllers or domineering and so cause other members to shut down. Some families are just "too busy" to talk.

Whatever the situation may have been in our past, and whether we know how to communicate well or not, the fact remains—talking to one another is critical to relationships. If we want our relationships to be good, then we will want to sharpen our communication skills and systems.

With the busy schedules of today's families, family meetings can offer an excellent forum for good communication. Jane Nelson, Ed.D., offers a detailed description for family meetings in her book, *Positive Discipline*.[2] Nelson suggests weekly meetings where issues are discussed and decisions are made by consensus whenever possible. A chairperson leads the meeting, working from an agenda (agenda items are submitted throughout the previous week by any family member). A secretary keeps notes, listing decisions, logging calendar items, and registering topics for the next week's meeting.

To keep the meetings positive, Nelson advises a compliment or gratitude exchange where each family member gives other members a compliment or words of appreciation. The next items on the agenda are problem solving, planning activities, and discussion of chores. Each meeting ends on a positive note by planning a fun, family activity for the coming week.

We started having family meetings in 1992. Our first goal was to establish the family meeting time as a positive, non-threatening occasion for our two boys. I prepared notebooks for each of us which included an agenda, blank calendar pages, and notebook paper. We talked about chores, repairs needed around the house, activities for scheduling and coordination, and dinner menus. Then we encouraged the boys to add their own topics. After the first few meetings, everyone felt comfortable and we moved on to "touchier" issues.

Establishing the safe environment for our family meetings was critical to their success. We look forward to our meetings, and all of us realize how important they are for our family life together. We try to have our meetings every Wednesday night after dinner dishes are finished, although during the summer we hold them on an as-needed basis. Now that school is back in swing, we're on our schedule again.

While our weekly meetings have improved our family communications, Fred and I still found we needed more time as husband and wife, mom and dad.

Couples' conferences. Couples with children know how difficult it is to find time to talk. Our friends Chris and Jeff Trautman encountered that problem after their two daughters, Sara and Rachel, were born. "Jeff and I used to have a lot of time to ourselves," Chris explained. "But when our girls were toddlers and requiring so much of my attention, Jeff and I realized we didn't have time to talk about things we needed to discuss."

So Chris and Jeff started meeting over breakfast at a restaurant one morning each week. They talked about financial matters, compared and coordinated calendars, planned vacation and family outings, and discussed other family business. Their first meeting was more than fifteen years ago, and Chris and Jeff found their time so essential that they've continued their weekly ritual to this day. "This isn't a time to talk about our relationship or deal with emotional issues," Chris told me. "We find that it's important to have a special time set aside to talk about all the details involved in running a household."

Parent summit meetings. Several times each year, Fred and I find it helpful to set aside an hour or so to discuss each of our children. We call these our parent summit meetings. During our meeting we look at the specific and unique needs of each child and develop a plan. We discuss our parenting skills, areas we need to strengthen, and techniques we've tried. We also divide the parenting duties, taking into account our own abilities, schedules, and desires. We both see our parent summit meetings as important as we continue the work of rearing our children and as we build positive, trusting relationships with them.

Date nights. The pattern is common: couples date, fall in love, go steady (date no one else), become engaged (do everything together—joined at the hip), get married (enjoy creating their new life together), have children, and rarely look into the whites of each other's eyes until they're empty nesters and ask, "Now, who are you?"

Fred and I often find ourselves longing for a time-out from our schedules and all the responsibilities of parenting, working, managing, and the list goes on. Following the cue of our friends Rich and Karmann, we started having date nights.

We're not up to the weekly outings (although that's a goal), but several times each month Fred and I go out and have fun together. Sometimes we meet friends, but most times it's just the two of us. We go to professional sporting events, dinner, or movies. Sometimes we'll just browse in bookstores, take a drive in the countryside, or visit a park. The activity isn't as important as being together as a couple. Date nights help keep the fires burning.

Annual planning meetings. Fred and I learned the incredible value of planning for our lives during our Lake Chelan getaway that I described earlier. I mention it here because it's a key element in our overall communication. These planning meetings set the direction for our goals and activities for the year ahead and into the future. Refer to chapter four and plan for your annual planning meeting.

One-on-ones. Good communication is more than talking. We also do a lot of things together which communicate the way we feel about one another, the importance of our relationships, and the high value we place on our family. One of the greatest communication techniques we use with our boys is our frequent and planned one-on-ones. Fred and I plan for these on our own and we both try to keep them spontaneous, yet intentional by making sure we follow through.

One-on-ones aren't weekly dates or scheduled meetings. Instead they're Dawit and me walking to the neighborhood bakery for a cookie and a cup of tea, or Seth and I going to see Nolan Ryan pitch for his last time against the Mariners. One-on-ones are how our family works out our belief that love is a verb. We *communicate* our commitment to one another by *doing*.

GET YOUR BANK TO PAY YOUR BILLS FOR YOU!

One of my most hated jobs is paying bills. I'm not sure why this monthly chore has turned into such a dreaded task—maybe it's because I hate seeing the hard-earned dollars leave without so much as a whimper and with such lightning speed. Maybe because bill-paying is so perpetual—month after month, year after year.

While I haven't figured out a way to get rid of bill-paying altogether, one thing I've done has helped reduce the amount of time and energy I put into the job. Maybe it will help you, too.

List all the bills you pay every month (mortgages, auto loans, consumer loans, etc.). Send a letter to each lender requesting an automatic payment. Give them your name, address, daytime phone number, loan number, amount of payment, your bank name and address, the account number and type (checking, savings, etc.) from which you want the funds drawn, and the date each month that you would like the transaction to take place (I have ours scheduled five days AFTER payday).

On the day the funds are to be drawn, make sure you have money available and that you write the transaction in your register. You can also do the same with utility bills and other monthly payments, even though the amount isn't the same each month.

Go to your banker and see what options are available. Banks are merging the needs of today's busy families with technological advances and are coming up with some great services. Electronic banking also curtails your chances of theft and forgery, a growing problem in our country.

The front end investment of time and money to set up this time- and stress-saving system will provide you with hours to read, visit with friends, walk, or even sleep! Streamlining your monthly bill-paying is another step out of the rat race.

TAMING THE PAPER MONSTER

I wanted to pass this tip along because it's made such a difference in my life. I am frequently boggled by the amount of paper flowing through and getting stuck in our household! Between my home business and our personal business, mail, magazines, and newspapers, I handle hundreds of pieces of paper every week. Just to survive the daily onslaught of paper through our door, I had to develop an easy and consistent plan. It's very basic and *it works!*

My desk has five places where papers can go:

1. *Wastebasket*—(this is always my first choice and I only settle for an alternative when absolutely necessary).

2. *To-File Basket*—a large wire basket on the floor under my desk where I toss all papers that must be permanently or temporarily filed. I sort and file the papers only when I can no longer fit any more papers in the basket.

In December of 1976 my house was destroyed by fire. While I had insurance, I didn't have a detailed list of material assets. Therefore, we had to sift through the charred possessions, write down every item we came across, along with an estimated value, and then turn our lists into the insurance company. After several weeks of work, we were able to prove that the fire destroyed the minimum amount of goods to receive the maximum amount of reimbursement.

If only I had gone around the house with a camera, I could have saved hours of awful work. Today, many homeowners have video cameras which make the process of recording belongings even more complete. Walk through each room of your home and film the artwork, furniture, special belongings, jewelry, electronic equipment, etc. As you film, talk about the items, where they were purchased, the approximate date of purchase, and the estimated value. If you don't have a video camera, do the same with a cassette recorder as you snap pictures with your camera.

Keep this valuable record someplace other than your home! In a safety deposit box, at your office, even in your car. Learn by my mistake. And don't wait... it really can happen to you.

3. *To-Pay Tray*—bills and bank statements go in one of two stacked trays on my desk. I handle this business only once each week by paying bills and balancing checking accounts.

4. *To-Do Tray*—if I need to write a letter, make a call, read a document, or take some other action, it goes in this tray, which I try to empty once each week after paying bills.

5. *Handy File Rack*—I have a slanted vertical organizer on my desk which holds labeled file folders. I have one file for each member of the family as well as several other files (church, newsletter, family meeting, banking, current projects, postage). These files are easily accessible, at my fingertips, and it's easy to drop correspondence, messages, and other pieces of paper into them.

As soon as I have mail or other papers, I place them in one of the five areas. If I'm in a hurry and can't sort the papers immediately, I stack them in the middle of my desk so I can't do another thing until they are properly sorted. This plan really works for me! I've tried several and it's the easiest, most consistent and most efficient.

I hate to file! In fact, I will put it off until I absolutely have no other choice (which is usually choosing between getting my work done or going mad).

In spite of my aversion to filing, I have an excellent system. I first started this system after reading *Financial Self-Defense* by Charles J. Givens. The book includes a list of files to help people store important documents that may be needed at a later date.

Since then, I've revised Givens' system and find it nearly foolproof. Though I hate filing and put it off until the very last minute, I can almost always go straight to my office and find any piece of paper I need to retrieve. Here's how you can set up a system for your use:

Go to a discount office supply store and purchase any of the following items you don't already have:

2-drawer file cabinet that is set up to hold hanging files

50 regular-sized hanging files

50 regular-sized manila file folders

50 clear-acetate labels for hanging files

1 box of self-adhesive file folder labels

Design your system on paper first. List the major categories you will use for your hanging files (see suggestions below, major categories are in CAPS). Then choose names for the files that will be placed in each of those categories. Here is a suggested checklist to begin your filing system. Select those file names that are appropriate for your use. Add other files you will need. The name of the file is shown in *italics*. The items that go in the file are listed after each name.

One of the primary causes of stress is sensing a loss of control. To prevent stress from souring a special family time, a holiday celebration, or a particular event, plan ahead.

First list the major tasks that must be accomplished to make the occasion a success, such as dining, gifts, decorations, invitations, etc.

Target the date of the event on your calendar, then work backwards to schedule when you need to complete each task.

Write each task on a notecard or a sheet of paper. Under the task, write the specific steps that you need to take, along with the date and the time each item should be started and completed.

This process enables you to maximize your control and therefore reduce your stress. It's a great way to insure fun celebrations and warm memories.

FAMILY

Children's File—a file or set of files for each child for school papers, report cards, mementos, awards, certificates

Christmas—gift lists, addresses for mailing cards, planning schedules, ideas

Church/Faith—Sunday School information, seminar brochures, pastor's name and telephone number, committee involvement, tithing records

Education—PTA information, viewbooks, college plans, night school, correspondence school, work-related courses

FINANCES

Asset Management Account—monthly statements, prospectuses

Bank Accounts—monthly statements, correspondence

Bills—payment books for bills that must be paid each month, bills that must be paid in the future (car insurance, licenses, etc.)

Credit Bureau Report—records, correspondence

Credit Card Bills/Receipts—a file for each card with monthly statements, correspondence

Financial History—net worth worksheets, spending plans from previous years

Investments, Annuities—records

Investments, IRA Accounts—records

Investments, Miscellaneous—records

Investments, Mutual Funds—records

Investments, Real Estate—records

Investments, Stock and Bond Certificates—records

Mortgage—purchase contract, mortgage agreement

Receipts—miscellaneous (only those that must be saved)

Taxes, Federal—tax-deductible receipts, tax returns, and files for last seven years (one file for each year)

Taxes, State—tax-deductible receipts, tax returns, and files for last seven years (one file for each year)

Utilities—electric, gas, water, sewer, telephone bills

HEALTH

Dental/Orthodontist Records—family dentist, address, phone number, bills, correspondence

Diets—diet plans for weight loss and health you have found successful for you

Doctor and Hospital Bills—family doctor, address, phone number, bills, correspondence

Medical Records—medical records, immunization records

HOME

Computer—hardware and software purchase contracts, guarantees, licenses, documentation

Guarantees, Warranties and Instructions—instructions and guarantees for carpets, tires, stereo equipment, appliances, electronic devices

Home Improvements—remodeling ideas, receipts

Leases—Lease and rental agreements for dwelling, appliances, etc.

IMPORTANT PAPERS

Birth Certificates—originals and copies for each member of the family

Diplomas—diplomas from high schools, colleges and universities, certificates of study

Driving—copy of current driver's license

Legal Documents—names and addresses of attorneys, divorce and property settlements, other legal matters

Marriage Certificates—original and copies

Passports—current and expired passports, visa photos, health cards

Titles—proof of ownership titles to cars, real estate, etc.

Will—original and copies, names and addresses of attorneys, living will information

INSURANCE

Insurance, Auto—insurance policy, insurance quotes, correspondence, traffic infractions and accidents, license plate information

Insurance, Health—health insurance policy and documentation

Insurance, Homeowner's—homeowner's or tenant's insurance policy, umbrella liability policy, personal property inventory list

Insurance, Life—life insurance policies, correspondence with company, insurance quotes

MEMORIES

Correspondence—letters and cards from friends and family

Paraphernalia—expired driver's licenses, documents

PLANNING

Financial Blueprint—your dreams, values and goals list, income and expense chart, savings chart

Retirement Plan—papers relating to your employment or small business retirement plan

Spending Plan—your planning sheets for how you will manage your money

RECREATION

Clubs—health club, country club, business club, book club, investment club

Hobbies—craft files, ideas

Sports—schedules, season ticket contracts

Vacations—vacation ideas

TRAVEL

Maps—maps to frequently visited locations, directions to hard-to-find homes of friends or other places

Frequent Flyer Clubs—award checks, statements

WORK

Employment Records—employment contract, employee handbook, benefits information, retirement plan information

Resumé—copies of your resumés, how-to's and ideas for good formats

After choosing the *categories* to meet your needs, make hanging file labels for each one, attach the labels to the hanging files, and place them in the top drawer of your file cabinet. After choosing the *file names* for each category, make a file folder label for each, attach the labels to the file folders, and sort them into the appropriate hanging file.

Begin sorting your documents into the appropriate folders. Make new categories and files when you find it necessary. At the beginning of the new year, sort through your files and toss any documents that no longer need saving. Set aside documents and receipts for income tax preparation. Move all your files to the bottom drawer and make a new set of files for the new year (keep your IMPORTANT PAPERS section in the current year drawer). After your second year of using this system, merely shift the contents of the hanging files to the appropriate hanging files in the bottom drawer which now serves as your long-term, permanent record file. Reuse the category files and make new file folders.

YOUR TURN

1. Review this chapter. Set up the systems that will help you save time and money. Again, the front-end investment will be multiplied over and over again!

11

The Send-Off

Well, friend, I hope you gained a sense of hope and excitement for your future as you learned of my journey out of the rat race. I'm not at the end of my trail yet. Occasionally I still get too busy, tired, or stressed. My house wouldn't survive the white-glove test and I'm not at my perfect weight. But my life is happier than it's ever been. I treasure each member of my family and thank God I can be with them. I love my friends and cherish our times together. I value my gifts and feel blessed to use them to communicate with others as they continue their life journey.

As you make your final preparations for your escape out of the rat race, I encourage you to take along a few other items:

1. *Out of the Rat Race* monthly newsletter. Readers tell me this is their *support group on paper*. You'll find inspirational articles, time- and money-saving tips, planning and organizing advice, and much more. Subscribe by sending your name, address, and a check or money order for $12 to: *Out of the Rat Race*, P.O. Box 95341, Seattle, WA 98145-2341.

2. *The Bottomline Personal.* This is a great bi-weekly newsletter, packed with advice on financial planning, communication skills, business tips, personal and business planning, and lifestyle issues. To subscribe, send your name, address, and a

165

check or money order for $49 to: *The Bottomline Personal,* P.O. Box 58446, Boulder, CO 80322.

3. *Making the Most of Your Money* **by Jane Bryant Quinn.** Published by Simon & Schuster and available at bookstores.

4. *Your Money or Your Life* **by Joe Dominguez and Vicki Robin.** Published by Viking in hard and soft covers, available at bookstores.

As we prepare to part company, I want to reproduce for you an excerpt from my personal journal. I think it embodies what we want from our lives—no matter how long or how brief they may be:

> Today I attended the memorial service for Rhonda Fleming Bast, the younger sister of my close friend. Rhonda, while a vibrant and active woman, couldn't match the cancer that had laid claim to her body for the last several years. She turned forty only a few months ago, and her early death left many of us stunned, questioning, and hurting.
>
> As friends and relatives shared their memories of Rhonda, they tried to wrap words around the sweet and gentle soul who had touched their lives. Her best friend Patty Ann stood at the podium, fighting back tears as she recalled Rhonda, "She always made whoever she talked with feel important. She taught me how to appreciate people—without regard for what they did or didn't own or for what position they had or didn't have. Rhonda taught me that everyone, no matter what, is valuable... she made me feel special and was always there to be my friend. I will miss her so much."
>
> While we are glad Rhonda is no longer suffering from her illness, we ache for the tremendous void now remaining for her husband, her teenage stepson, and her four-year-old little boy. I pray for comfort for them, Rhonda's parents, her

brothers and sister-in-law, and for her many friends.

Tonight, as I replay in my mind the afternoon and the comments of those who loved and cared for Rhonda and her family, I realize how the death of a loved one can raise our awareness of the bare reality of life. How, perhaps, it is good to remind ourselves of that starkness more often and at times other than memorial services.

It is in death's shadow that we realize how very fragile life can be. It is at times like these that we reconsider what is most important in our lives. We think of the tremendous value we place on our loved ones.

We are reminded that what is truly precious cannot be purchased at a department store... or awarded at an annual review. That people, not things, provide love. And that friends, not positions, provide comfort and companionship.

When confronted with the reality of death's finality, we make promises to ourselves to be better spouses, better parents, better friends, and better people. To work less and to play more. To complain less and to love more. And to try, once again, to keep what is truly most important in our hearts, first in our everyday lives.

The good news is that Rhonda Fleming Bast had a husband who treasured her and a son who felt treasured by her. She lived a life filled with love, joy, and laughter.

The bad news is that Rhonda was unable to live her life as long as she or we wanted. Nonetheless, we are grateful for the time she was with us, for the love we shared, and for the example she modeled as we who remain carry on our lives and try to keep the promises we made this day.

Listen to the promises you've made to yourself. Do whatever you need to keep them. You have what it takes to begin your journey toward a lifestyle that encourages your growth and cultivates fulfillment. Fulfill your hopes. Reach your dreams. I know you can do it. With confidence in you, I bid you farewell and wish you the best, my friend.

Happy trails to you, until we meet again....

Notes

ONE
Getting Out of the Rat Race

1. Joe Dominguez, *Transforming Your Relationship with Money and Achieving Financial Independence*, audiotape course, (Seattle: New Road Map Foundation, 1986).
2. Sue Bender, *Plain and Simple* (San Francisco: HarperSan Francisco, a division of HarperCollins, 1989), 4.

TWO
The Unveiling

1. Victor E. Frankl, *Emphasis on Faith and Living*, August 1981, 5, as quoted in Albert M. Wells, Jr., *Inspiring Quotations* (Nashville: Thomas Nelson Publishers, 1988), 109.
2. Carl Jung, from M. Scott Peck, *Further Along the Road Less Traveled* (New York: Simon & Schuster, 1993), 174.
3. From William J. Bennett, *The Index of Leading Cultural Indicators* (New York: A Touchstone Book published by Simon & Schuster, 1994), 102.
4. Margaret Craven, *I Heard the Owl Call My Name* (Garden City, N.Y.: Doubleday, 1973), Part III, Chapter 16.
5. Anne Frank, *The Diary of a Young Girl* (New York: F. Watts, 1954), Entry 6 July 1944.
6. Victor E. Frankl, works include *Man's Search for Meaning* (Boston: Beacon Press, 1962); *The Doctor and the Soul* (New York: A.A. Knopf, 1965); and *The Unconscious God* (New York: Simon & Schuster, 1975).
7. *Emphasis on Faith and Living*, August 1981, 5, as quoted in Albert M. Wells, Jr., *Inspiriting Quotations* (Nashville: Thomas Nelson Publishers, 1988), 109.

THREE
It's a Matter of Principles

1. Alan Bennett, *Beyond the Fringe* (New York: Random House, 1963) from *The Macmillan Dictionary of Quotations* (New York: Macmillan Publishing Company, 1989), 323.
2. Ralph Waldo Emerson, *Banner*, 11 March 1977, 5, as quoted in Albert M. Wells, Jr., *Inspiring Quotations* (Nashville: Thomas Nelson Publishers, 1988), 13.
3. Thomas Jefferson, as compiled by H. Jackson Brown, Jr., *A Father's Book of Wisdom* (Nashville: Rutledge Hill Press, 1988), 23.
4. Linda and Richard Eyre, *Teaching Your Children Values* (New York: Fireside Book by Simon & Schuster Publishers, 1992), 13.
5. Stephen R. Covey, *The Seven Habits of Highly Effective People* (New York: Fireside Book by Simon & Schuster Publishers, 1989), 18.
6. Helen Keller, as quoted in H. Jackson Brown, Jr., *A Father's Book of Wisdom* (Nashville: Rutledge Hill Press, 1988), 22.
7. Alan Scholes, "The Church/State Puzzle in the Soviet Classroom," *Christianity Today* (Carol Stream, Ill.: November 25, 1991), 22.

FOUR
Uncovering Your Life Equation

1. William Temple, *Pentecostal Evangel*, Feb. 29, 1976, as quoted in Albert M. Wells, Jr., *Inspiring Quotations* (Nashville: Thomas Nelson Publishers, 1988), 215.
2. Søren Kierkegaard, from the editor's files, *Ibid*, 109.
3. William Temple, *Pentecostal Evangel*, Feb. 29, 1976, as quoted in Albert M. Wells, Jr., *Inspiring Quotations* (Nashville: Thomas Nelson Publishers, 1988), 215.
4. Roy Disney, as quoted in H. Jackson Brown, Jr., *A Father's Book of Wisdom* (Nashville: Rutledge Hill Press, 1988), 131.
5. Gary Smalley, *Joy That Lasts* (Grand Rapids, Mich.: Zondervan, 1986), 23.
6. Claude Brown, "When Did Kids Turn Killers?", *Los Angeles Times*, May 22, 1988, Section: Issues, page A14.
7. Br. Abraham, "At St. Johns," *Abbey Letter*. St. Gregory's Abbey, Three Rivers, Mich., Fall 1993.
8. Matthew 11:28, author's paraphrase.
9. Bruce Larson and Keith Miller, *Edge of Adventure* (Waco, Tex.: Word Books, 1974).
10. Paula Peisner, *Finding Time* (Naperville, IL: Sourcebooks Trade, 1992), 91.

FIVE
Writing Your Personal Mission Statement

1. Covey, *The Seven Habits of Highly Effective People*, 106.
2. Bender, *Plain and Simple*, 145.

SIX
How Much Is Enough?

1. Ralph Larson, *These Times*, July 1980, as quoted in Albert M. Wells, Jr., *Inspiring Quotations* (Nashville: Thomas Nelson Publishers, 1988), 128.
2. Alexander Solzhenitsyn, *Humanist*, Jan.-Feb. 1979, as quoted in Albert M. Wells, Jr., *Inspiring Quotations*, (Nashville: Thomas Nelson Publishers, 1988), 129.
3. Ivan Illich, *Tools for Conviviality* (New York: Harper & Row, 1971), as quoted in *The Macmillan Dictionary of Quotations* (New York: Macmillan Publishing Company, 1989), 355.
4. St. Francis of Assisi, *Little Flowers of St. Francis of Assisi*, as quoted in *The Treasury of Religious and Spiritual Quotations*, edited by Rebecca Davis and Susan Mesner, (Pleasantville, N.Y.: Reader's Digest Association, Inc., 1994), 529.

SEVEN
Here I Am

1. Joe Dominquez and Vicki Robin, *Your Money or Your Life* (New York: Viking, 1992), 20, of the prologue.
2. Jane Bryant Quinn, *Making the Most of Your Money*, (New York: Simon & Schuster, 1991).
3. Reinhold Niebuhr, from *The Twelve Steps for Christians* (San Diego, Calif.: Recovery Publications, 1988), 120.

EIGHT
Get a Grip

1. Public Health Service
2. John Capri, "Relieving the Strain of Stress," *Medical World News*, May 1993, 22.
3. Br. Abraham, "At St. Johns," *Abbey Letter*. St. Gregory's Abbey, Three Rivers, Mich., Fall 1993.

4. George Sweeting shared this management tool with Fred and me at a conference we attended where he was the guest speaker.
5. Marcus Tullius Cicero (106-43 B.C.) as quoted in Norman Vincent Peale, *My Favorite Quotations* (San Francisco: HarperSan Francisco, a division of Harper-Collins Publishers, 1991), 126.

NINE
Your Personal Escape Route

1. Jane Bryant Quinn, "What's Your Debt Limit," *Woman's Day*, 23 November 1993, 22.
2. Jo Robinson and Jean Coppock Staeheli, *Unplug the Christmas Machine* (New York: Quill, 1982), 19.

TEN
Packing the Essentials

1. Natasha Toufexis, "Drowsy America," *Time Magazine*, December 17, 1990, 78.
2. Toufexis, "Drowsy America," 78.
3. Toufexis, "Drowsy America," 78.
4. Jane Nelson, Ed.D., *Positive Discipline* (Fair Oaks, Calif.: Sunrise Press, 1981), 144.